The Ben Lilly Legend

T H E
Ben Lilly Legend

by J. FRANK DOBIE

UNIVERSITY OF TEXAS PRESS
Austin

International Standard Book Number 978-0-292-70728-3
Library of Congress Catalog Number 80-53428

Eleventh University of Texas Press printing, 2012

Reprinted by arrangement with Little, Brown and
Company, Inc.

Requests for permission to reproduce material from this
work should be sent to:
Permissions
University of Texas Press
P.O. Box 7819
Austin, TX 78713-7819
www. utpress.utexas.edu/index.php/rp-form

♾ The paper used in this book meets the minimum
requirements of ANSI/NISO Z39.48-1992 (R1997)
(Permanence of Paper).

Contents

Esau the Hunter

FOR generations stretching back to the horizon of chronicled time, the hairy one called Esau has been held up as a sermon against improvidence, thriftlessness, surrender to appetite, foolish evaluation of the offerings that life makes.

Esau was a cunning hunter, a man of the woods and field. He could read sign; he knew all the shepherd lore about weeds, snails and stars. Walls cramped him; cushions smothered him; the smallness of small people wilted him. Only out in the open could he expand. "Canst thou bind the sweet influences of Pleiades, or loose the bands of Orion?"

His twin brother Jacob was cunning too — cunning in getting and holding. He never went hunting, but dwelt about the tents, where he kept tally on every lamb added to the estate and on every ephah of wheat advanced to a servant. His old father Isaac loved Esau, saw in him the vanished strength and freedom of his own youth, delighted in the wild taste of the venison he brought home. The mother of the boys loved Jacob and took pride in the way he saved, hoarded pieces of string, and spied on the hirelings. Jacob would some day sit in the seats of the mighty, and God would listen for his advice — given in the form of humble prayer, of course — on how to run the country.

One winter morning, long before daylight, Esau went out to hunt. He was making for a hollow on the other side of the last line of hills. He did not need sun or stars or wind to course by; something inside him was as true as a compass. He did not see the sun that morning. A bitter wind driving rain blew up against him at dawn. He knew it would send the deer into coverts, but he kept on going. He crawled through mud, slid on rocks, crept through brush. Water dripped from his eyebrows. By the time he turned homewards his feet were leaded and his soaked clothes weighed like a heavy drag.

At night when he came in, empty-handed, he was trembling with cold and hunger. Nothing makes a man so hollow as walking all day, sodden and chilled to the marrow, in biting wind and rain. As he dragged into the warm, lighted tent, he smelled the stew that Jacob had been comfortably and calculatingly seething. He was so faint that he reeled. Every fiber in his being called out for the steaming nourishment, as cracked soil yearns for moisture. He was a part of the good earth.

And Esau said to Jacob, "Feed me, I pray thee, with that same red pottage . . . I am faint."

And Jacob said, "Convey to me thy birthright, and I will give you to eat."

And Esau said, "Behold I am at the point to die. What profit shall my birthright do to me unless I eat?"

And Jacob said, "Swear to me this day."

And Esau sware away his birthright for something to eat.

Then Jacob gave Esau bread and pottage of lentiles; and he did eat and drink, and rose up, and went his way.

The years passed and Jacob, going his way, gained property and power. He cheated his father-in-law, schemed to circumvent nature, and became the model for all graspers after unearned increments that the world has since rewarded. He became the upholder of all respectabilities and was the main pillar of society. He advanced the orthodoxy of all royalists of all times: *Keep on top by keeping others down.* When he gave a gift it was to win a favor. When in the stillness of evening he heard the chirp of crickets, he wondered if the shepherds of his far-spread flocks were listening against wolves. When he gave a farthing to a blind singer of ballads, he silently accused him of shiftlessness. The ballad bore no meaning for him.

And the way that Esau went was still the way of the hunter, over the hills and far away, the sun and the rain in his face, free from the bondages of property, free from the gnawing lust to possess everything he saw and to outsmart all his fellow men. He did not consider himself wise enough to give God much advice. Yet he was no shiftless rabbit-hunter of Rip Van Winkle irresponsibility with an outcast cur for his only respecter. Despite Jacob's craftiness and his own appetite, he had tents, family and flocks. He owned things, but things did not own him. On warm spring days he could lie on the grass and listen to it grow and receive a joy beyond that of watching his own sheep fatten on it or of wanting, like Nebuchadnezzar, to eat it himself. When the wind blew fresh, he could sniff it and gladden within himself at how the old does were sniffing it too and working their ears and nostrils. He could stretch out for hours on the ground, his back to a log, watching over a valley, the light clouds drifting one way, the cawing ravens flying another, and, thus lingering, feel something sweet and clarifying to his soul, a kind of liberation, seep into him. He gazed into spring dawnings to hear the lark's faltering notes come dropping down. In his heart he thanked every ballad singer that he heard. Jacob said he was childish; Rachel said he was childlike; his nephew Joseph and other boys thought him a hero. He presaged another treader of the open lands who long afterwards liked to lie down in green pastures and wait by still waters and who sang a song: "I will lift up mine eyes unto the hills."

In time Esau grew too wobbly in the knees to follow a trail, too weak in muscle to draw a bow, too watery in the eyes to pick out the flick of a stag's antler in the bush. Like his father Isaac before him, though, he still craved strong venison and remembered free days with the wild things. Poet Whitney Montgomery has pictured "Esau Grown Old." *

> Make room for him
>   By the fireplace;
> He is done with the hunt,
>   He is done with the chase.
>
> He is done with the hills
>   And the torrent's thunder
> And the deep, dark woods
>   That he loved to wander.

* Quoted by permission of author and publisher from *Hounds in the Hills,* by Whitney Montgomery, The Kaleidograph Press, Dallas, Texas, 1934.

The Ben Lilly Legend

CHAPTER I

Mister Ben Lilly and His Book

LATE in January, 1928, I was in El Paso on the Rio Grande listening to stories about the Lost Tayopa Mine in Sonora and the gold and golden oranges of El Naranjal somewhere — nobody knows exactly where — in Sinaloa. While I was outfitting to go down into Chihuahua and make a pack trip across the Sierra Madre on the Tayopa trail, the American National Livestock Association held its annual convention in the city.

Among the New Mexicans who thronged in was Victor Culberson, manager and part owner of the far-spread G O S ranch, a pillar to the Association, and a picturesque character willing to pay for additions to picturesqueness. At an afternoon session he introduced Ben V. Lilly to talk on predatory animals. He told how Mr. Lilly, after having been engaged to kill panthers and bears off the G O S range, walked to headquarters leading a burro loaded with all his worldly possessions and straightway wanted to know

[3]

how much pasturage he should pay. According to range custom, grass for an employee's private mount is as free as water for the owner. Mr. Lilly had agreed to hunt and trap on a bounty basis, boarding himself, but nothing had been said about his burro. "Nothing for the grass, hell, nothing," Vic Culberson told him. But, no, Mr. Lilly would not take more than had been stipulated; he would not rest until it was settled that fifteen cents a month for the burro's pasturage be taken out of his bounty money — which was a hundred dollars per grown predator.

Vic Culberson went on to tell how if the old hunter's dogs treed a mountain lion on Saturday night, they had to guard it until Monday morning. He would not shoot or do any work whatsoever on the Day of Rest. He would leave the ranch with nothing but a tin can or a frying pan, twenty-five pounds of meal, some salt, his ax, rifle and dogs, and not come back until he ran out of lion tracks, maybe two weeks later. What most people consider ordinary comforts, he regarded as debilitating luxuries; even at ranch headquarters, in the dead of winter as well as in summer softness, he camped out. He had been hunting all his life, from east to west, and knew more about the wild animals than any other man in the mountains. We could depend upon every word he told us as being true.

One look at the expression of unworldly goodness and truth on Mr. Lilly's serene face confirmed the judgment. He was at that time seventy-one years old, though common talk put him at eighty and past. He stood up, stumpily built, firm-footed, eyes as clear and blue and fresh as a Western sky after a June rain, and a kind of British sea captain complexion that glowed above his Santa Claus beard. His voice was so soft and his whole expression so innocent that nobody listening to him and looking at him for the first time would suspect the emphasis and stubbornness he kept in reserve.

This was the first public speech he had ever made, except for a talk to a Sunday School class. He said he "had rather be off in the woods and wild," but he had learned things there that other people do not know. If a man did not get some education tracking a wild animal, he had better go home and plow. For towards an hour he talked about bears and panthers. His talk was altogether devoid of those tedious details about going north up one hollow, across a mountain to the west, thence southeast into timber, and so on, characteristic of many hunter narratives — details that by comparison make the abstracts of land titles thrilling reading. Everything he said reflected a minute familiarity with animal ways and spaces beyond man-made trails. While he talked he was collected and was

"Property is a handicap to man," he announced calmly.

I told him of Henry David Thoreau's going off to live in austerity by a lake in the woods and saying that "a man is rich in proportion to the number of things he can do without."

"That is a fine phrase," he responded. "You are a bright young man to think of it. I like to live out, because people and houses keep me from thinking and being myself."

"You are like Emerson," I commented. "He said that society is in conspiracy against the individual."

"That is better than I could say the thing," he added. "It makes me understand better what is meant by polishing the language. . . .

"When I am around babies," he went on, "I always tote them out on my arm in the evening and let them look at the stars and feel the wind. They sleep better for that. They would sleep better still if they had their pallets on the ground. I always sleep better on the ground. Something agreeable to my system seeps into it from the ground.

"Every man and woman ought to get out and be alone with the elements a while every day, even if only for five minutes. I can't think at all except when I am out. I like to think of the past. I can think of myself as a barefooted boy standing before the fireplace with my hands spread out, and of my mother close by me, and I am happy. I cannot be happy trying to grasp the future, unless it's something like a lion that I am trailing."

Much of what he told me about the panthers and bears he had hunted is scattered through the chapters of this book. This was the subject that he came back to after any philosophical diversion. He had been born with a talent for hunting, he said, "and if we are not faithful to our talents, we lose them."

" 'That one talent which is death to hide,' " I put in.

"Who said that?" he asked.

"John Milton."

"I heard of him when I was a boy. He was a famous Christian."

He kept alluding to the black bears he had killed in the canebrakes of Louisiana, to the grizzlies he had tracked to their doom in New Mexico and Arizona, and the big ones he had got down in Mexico. He was as strong on panthers as on bears. He treasured with great pride an article written by Teddy Roosevelt on a hunt with him in Louisiana. Finally, I asked him how many bears he had killed.

"That's a secret I am keeping for my book," he replied.

At that time *Trader Horn* was a popular book, and when I told Mr. Lilly that his experiences and philosophy might be woven into as good a book as Trader Horn's he was delighted. He wanted to know about Trader Horn. "I'm writing a book," he said after a short silence, and then I let him know that I was a writer. Up to that moment he had regarded me as one of the cattlemen, though oddly tinctured with book-reading. Never having concerned himself with the affairs of other people, he was not nearly so skillful in detecting occupational marks on men as in reading bear sign. A man interested in writing was a new continent to him. He had something, he said, that he would like to show me, and suggested that we go over to the old Shelton Hotel, where he had a room.

I was stopping there too. The Shelton later burned down, to my regret, and was supplanted by a banal chain hotel. I recall it, even its cockroaches, with affection. It was peculiarly constructed, with two or three levels on each floor and with halls as full of turns as a mule trail down into a canyon of the Sierra Madre. When we reached the Shelton lobby, Mr. Lilly walked over to the desk and said something to the clerk. The clerk worked the combination to the lock on the door of a steel vault just back of the desk, opened the pon-

derous door, reached into a cavern that had hid for-
tunes in gold and silver smuggled across the Rio Bravo
in revolutionary times, and pulled out a sack that had
at one time been white and held forty-eight pounds of
XXXX flour. A knot was tied in the open end; the con-
tents were manifestly light.

Mr. Lilly took the flour sack, indicated that I was
to follow him, and led the way upstairs, around corners of the halls, over the up-and-down levels of his
floor, finally stopping at the door to Room 217. He
unlocked the door, opened it, and after we were inside, closed the door and relocked it. Then he opened
the flour sack and took out a typewritten manuscript
of perhaps twenty-five pages. Handing it to me, he
said, "You can read it." These were the first words
that had been spoken since his request of the hotel
clerk.

I took the manuscript, saw the title, *What I Know
about Bears*, felt for a chair, and read, utterly absorbed,
until I had reached the end. The concrete, firsthand
observations fascinated me. This was to be a chapter
in his proposed book. It was not written in a style that
any publisher would approve of, but when I was
through with it and we began to talk, I learned that
Mr. Lilly did not intend for any editor or publisher
to add a period or transpose a clause. He had had a

schoolteacher in a New Mexico mining camp copy it, he explained, and in his mild way he was incensed that she had made several changes in his punctuation and construction.

By the time I had finished reading *What I Know about Bears*, it was good dark. My host declined to eat supper with me. He would not so much as drink a cup of coffee. He never drank coffee, much less any kind of liquor. He let me know that he was not sleeping on the hotel bed but was spreading some of the bedclothes on the floor and sleeping there. He complained of the "rancid" air. If I would come back on the following evening, he said, he would let me read the second chapter of his book.

Late the next afternoon we met again, got the flour sack out of the vault, followed the meandering trail to his room, and were locked inside it once more. The title of the second chapter was *What I Know about Panthers*. I had in my coat pocket a copy of the *El Paso Times* containing a short account of Ben Lilly's address to the National Livestock Association on the preceding day, and a copy of the *Saturday Evening Post*. While I was taking a preliminary glance at the manuscript before settling into it, I thought of the newspaper and magazine and, reaching for them without looking up, said, "Mr. Lilly, perhaps you would like to read something here while I am reading what you have written."

"No, I thank you," he replied, and then in a voice of serene and settled conviction he added, "I find this very in-ter-est-ing."

I looked up at him. He was deeply immersed in *What I Know about Bears.*

He said nothing about the newspaper account of his talk, but I am sure that he had read it — and was better satisfied with himself than with the reporter. Not long after he got back to his camp he wrote J. B. Drake in Louisiana: "The shorthand writers failed to catch what I said. They got so interested they lost out."

The chapter on panthers contained, in addition to the author's original observations, a collection of tales he had heard about panther attacks on human beings. I was regretful that there was not a third — and a thirtieth — chapter to read.

Ben Lilly did not finish his book. The evidence is that he wrote no other chapter. As I was to learn, not long after he returned to the mountains from El Paso, he took pneumonia. He recovered but gradually declined. During his second childhood, two of my friends, one a rancher and the other a scout for walnut stumps, tried to locate the manuscripts for me. They learned nothing. Mr. Lilly died, but his shadow went on lengthening. The loss of his manuscripts seemed a wrong to his memory, and, aside from that, I wanted to make use of them.

In 1940, I wrote an article on him, emphasizing the lost manuscripts, and sent copies of it to the El Paso and two New Mexico newspapers. Dr. L. A. Jessen, dentist at Bayard, New Mexico, wrote: "Somewhere I have two articles by Ben Lilly, one on bears and one on lions, both in his fine hand, written with pencil on cheap tablet paper." I responded, asking to be allowed to copy them. Other men and women wrote me about Mr. Lilly, but I heard no more from Dr. Jessen.

One August day, towards three months after I had heard from him, I stepped into his office. "I haven't been able to locate them," were his first words. One of the articles he had loaned to somebody whose name was forgotten; the other was "probably" in a storeroom, in fragments. This storeroom was of adobe with a dirt floor. Lime, spilled from three or four sacks, was mixed with the papers and miscellaneous junk. Dr. Jessen's boys had gone through the papers more than once looking for old stamps, their energy evidently outrunning their sense of orderliness. The first leaf of Ben Lilly's penciled tablet that I found was numbered 32. Most of the leaves turned up separately. By the time I found the last leaf of the tablet, number 89, only four were missing. It was sundown and I could no longer breathe the lime-dusted air. I told the Jessen boys that I would be back in two or three days and would pay a quarter apiece for the missing leaves. They had them when I got back.

I went to see Harvey Forsythe at the Santa Rita copper mines a few miles away. He had hunted with Ben Lilly, had been made executor of the estate of the deceased Tom O'Brien, at whose ranch on the Mimbres River Ben Lilly had lived in his decline, and at this ranch had found, in addition to Lilly's diary for 1916, the chapters on bears and panthers, copied in ink in a neat Spencerian hand. Either mice or rats, however, had gnawed away about half of every page of the bear chapter. I now had two copies of the panther chapter, neither being the typewritten form I had read, but the pages on bears were too mutilated to be restored.

At the G O S ranch headquarters a cowboy helped me to excavate the bed of a disused wagon, under a brush shed, about a hundred yards from the house, in which Ben Lilly used to sleep. It was more than a foot deep in gunny sacks and straw, with empty patent medicine bottles and papers mixed in. I saved all the papers and found among them a letter from W. H. McFadden, of Ponca City, Oklahoma, thanking Mr. Lilly for a diary. I wrote Mr. McFadden. He responded from Fort Worth, to which he had moved, and sent me a carbon copy of the diary. He had given the original, along with numerous Lilly letters, to Monroe Goode, in Dallas.

Meanwhile, Tom Harp was writing me the equivalent of a small book on Lilly's career in Louisiana. On a trip I made to that state and to Mississippi, he guided me to various informants. Ben Lilly made these people, like scores whom I interviewed in New Mexico, Arizona and Texas, remember him concretely. I found that almost nobody referred to him as "Old Man Lilly," as "Old Lilly," or otherwise than with marked respect. To most rememberers he was, and is, either Mister Lilly or plain Ben Lilly.

Had Mister Ben Lilly written his book, this one would never have been begun. It was more than three-fourths completed when, in the fall of 1943, I flew to England to lecture for a year on American History at Cambridge University. I took the manuscript with me — and never looked at it. I have written and published two books since then. Now, twenty-one years after my one encounter with Ben Lilly, I still see his clear, serene eyes, as limpid as childhood's. The "power of harmony" had given them an open assurance, and in one way they seemed to hide nothing. Certainly they reflected nothing of design on other human beings. Yet in a strange way they seemed to shadow personal matters never to be revealed.

[15]

CHAPTER II

The Cowwhip

DESPITE many conflicting statements, his own included, as to the date, Benjamin Vernon Lilly was born December 31, 1856, in Wilcox County, Alabama. The family Bible says so. His parents were native to North Carolina. Margaret Anna McKay, his mother, was of Scotch ancestry, and when she married Albert Lilly on November 7, 1855, she was seventeen years old and had just graduated from Nicholson Female College, in Kemper County, Mississippi. Not long after Ben was born, his parents moved to Kemper County, and here his mother seems to have taught astronomy for a while in the "finishing school" of which she was a graduate. She could not be called learned, but she read books, especially the Bible; she had a strong mind, an energetic body and a wholesome nature. She and her husband believed in education sufficiently for one daughter to become a teacher in Davidson College and another a pipe-organist and music teacher. Before she died at the age of forty-nine ın Hazelhurst, Mississippi, where the family moved in 1878, she had borne seven children, the youngest being eight years old at the time. She herself was one of seven children, as was likewise her husband.

Before the Revolutionary War, William Lilly had come to North Carolina from England and taken up land among the Indians, out beyond the remotest settler. There in the wilderness he kept on wearing his wig and his gold knee-buckles. He was a little queer. A kinsman, John Lilly, silversmith and gunsmith, was so active in the Revolution that the Tories had a price on his head. The loss of a leg gave him the sobriquet of "Pegleg." The loss did not impede his making guns for fellow patriots. At times he had to hide among the boulders on Rocky River, and the figures of animals that he here carved on rocks remained long after he passed. On one occasion three British soldiers surprised him. "If I had two good feet, you would not take me," he said to them. "I believe I can whip you anyhow. Nellie, my sword!" Nellie obeyed quickly, but he was overcome and taken to Salisbury. The first night in prison, however, he escaped and then, on his pegleg, walked fifty miles back to his hiding-out grounds.

Steelwork was a family occupation. Benjamin Franklin Lilly, William's son, made guns famous for taking prizes at turkey shoots. He fought in the War of 1812.

His son Albert (1827–1906) was a wheelwright and blacksmith, and he joyously rode an "Arabian horse." During the Civil War he forged horseshoes and blades, his specialty being a kind of Roman sword — a stout blade, tapering to a point, eighteen inches long, sharp on both edges and provided with a cutlass-style handle. Into the blade, against the hilt, of this combination of hack-knife, sword and dagger, he always cut A. LILLY. Tempering the steel was his pride — a cherry red in the flame and a pigeon blue in the oil or water — if he did not have oil — in which he cooled it.

Albert Lilly's hero was General Nathan Bedford Forrest, and the sharp, strong, wieldy blade he wrought was the very knife for Forrest's hard-slashing, deadly-firing, hell-for-leather-riding men. No cavalryman ever believed more strongly in steel, hot or cold, than Bedford Forrest. During the four years of the Civil War, he with his own cavalry knife and "navy six" killed thirty Yankee fighting men in hand-to-hand combats — and had twenty-nine horses shot dead under him. "War means fighting, and fighting means killing," he said. Throughout life, Ben Lilly shared his father's admiration for Forrest — perhaps not so much for his fighting ways as for his extraordinary endurance, his unflagging pertinacity, his abstinence from tobacco and liquor, the fact of his being also a blacksmith's son, and, above all, his boyhood prowess in panther-killing.

During Ben Lilly's youth, Bedford Forrest's panther was still screaming over the tradition-remembering and story-telling South. In 1834, while Bedford was thirteen, the Forrests settled in the timbers and canebrakes of Mississippi, ten miles from the nearest neighbor. There were no roads, only horse trails. One morning Mrs. Forrest and her sister Fannie Beck, who lived with the family, rode to the neighbor's for a visit. When they started back late in the afternoon, their hostess presented Mrs. Forrest with a hatching of young chickens in a basket. A mile or so before they reached home the sun went down and the woods grew dusky.

Presently the silence was broken by the scream of a panther, unseen but only a few yards away in the dense woods. The excited horses broke into a run, Fannie Beck's in the lead. Fannie shouted back to her sister to drop the chickens and let the beast have them, but Mariam Forrest was not going to let any varmint have her chickens. On they raced, necessarily holding the horses back somewhat on the narrow, twisting, log-impeded trail. An occasional scream told that the panther was following. They reached the stream of deep, steep, slick banks just beyond which their cabin was located. Here they were compelled to slow down.

As they were descending, the panther leaped, its front claws tearing into Mrs. Forrest's side and neck, its hind claws into her horse's back and haunches. The plunging of the horse loosened the panther's hold and threw it into the water, but its claws had ripped Mrs. Forrest's clothes from her back and the flesh from her shoulders. The screams from the women brought thirteen-year-old Bedford and the other children from the cabin. When their mother descended from the saddle, she still held the basket of little chickens.

As soon as she was found to be only flesh-wounded and was made comfortable, young Forrest took his flintlock rifle down from the deerhorn rack above the fireplace and started towards the door.

"Son, where are you going at this time of night?" his mother asked.

"I am going to call the dogs and trail that panther and kill him if he stays on the earth."

She could not dissuade him. The trail would be cold by morning, he said. Away he went. The hounds soon picked up the scent, and until about midnight Bedford kept with them through briars, swamp and cane-brake. But the dogs were getting ahead of him and he feared they would run beyond his hearing. He cut a small grapevine, tied one end of it around the neck of an old hound to lead him. At times the other dogs were out of hearing, but the old hound followed true. Finally he heard them barking "treed." He had to wait for daylight to locate the panther up in the big white oak under which the dogs bayed. It was stretched out on a limb, lashing its long tail and softly snarling. He primed the pan of his flintlock afresh, aimed, and sent a bullet through the critter's heart. He got home with the scalp about nine o'clock.

In hunting down a beast of this character, a youth of impressionability might regard himself as a kind of Saint George after the Dragon. In Ben Lilly's mind, as we shall see, all panthers were dragons. Like many other men, he came to regard his own desire as a destiny imposed from on High. His deepest desire was to hunt. He hunted, and called hunting a patriotic duty.*

His uncle Vernon Lilly, for whom he was named, was a bachelor and well-to-do planter in Morehouse Parish, Louisiana. At the age of twelve Ben ran away from home and walked all the way to his uncle's, sleeping in the woods at night. He hunted for a while and then went back or was taken back to Mississippi. There were no public schools in the state at the time, South-

---

* "I told my wife that [fighting the Indians] was a duty I owed to my country. The truth is, my dander was up, and nothing but war could bring it right again." — *The Autobiography of David Crockett.*

erners regarding school taxes as a violation of their rights. His parents sent him to Jackson to a military academy — barely above a grade school in curriculum. He did not want to be schooled. For a long while Ben was lost to the family. This was the period of life that he later referred to as "wild." One day while on business in the city of Memphis, Vernon Lilly saw a sign over a blacksmith and machine shop — B. V. LILLY. He entered and told his young namesake that if he would come to his farm, settle down and marry, he would will him all his property.

The farm had around three hundred acres in cultivation, enclosed by rail fences. The remainder of the land was part of a great unfenced common of swamps, canebrakes and woods lying along the Bayou Bonne Idee, which merges with the wide-bottomed Boeuf River. The farmhouse consisted of two ample rooms divided by a wide hall, open at each end, a wide gallery running across the front of the house, and shed rooms built at the rear. The sills of this house might still serve as girders for bridging the Mississippi.

Here on this farm, which he eventually heired, and in the vast woodlands surrounding it, Ben Lilly grew to maturity and entered upon his far-stretched career of withdrawing into solitudes, hunting bears and panthers, observing wild life, keeping the Sabbath Day holy, preserving independence of body and mind, and cultivating eccentricities.

The country of his youth and pristine manhood was itself pristine, and unbelievably prolific in life. Some of the sparse settlers were still struggling to perfect the Spanish titles to the land. No railroad entered it until he was nigh forty years old. The old emigrant road to Texas snaked through the swamps and across the Mer Rouge Prairie of Morehouse Parish, and some of the travelers over it from Alabama, Georgia and elsewhere did not add to the placidity of the region. In one winter shortly before the Civil War a single hunting camp in the canebrakes of this parish killed seventy-five bears. When, years later, T. Y. Harp's father and mother began their married life on a small clearing in the heart of the great swamp, deer were so numerous that they had to be killed to save the crop on a twenty-acre field. Time and again Mark Harp killed as many as five deer in one day around his field. He would load deer carcasses on his wagon and give them away to people in the settlement.

Ben Lilly lived on the edge of a lush bottom eighty miles wide occasionally overflowed by the Mississippi River. Then, he could go to any spot in it in a skiff as well as at other times he could go afoot or on horse. He knew the woods so well and had such a sense of direction that he could on a drizzly day kill a deer in the middle of this forest-swamp, go on for hours over the trailless expanse, and then come directly back to the deer he had hung up. Going along with his head down, he knew where he was as definitely as if he were following a blazed trail. It was his boast that he could enter a pathless swamp in the middle of the night, stick his knife in any tree, come out, and the next night enter the swamp from any direction and go straight to the tree and reclaim the knife. He could back-trail himself like a range horse. His sense of direction was not based on a knowledge of the compass, on observation of land-marks, the stars, currents of air, or any other observ-able form of matter. It was inside of him; it was an instinct, like that of a bear or a pigeon — something more elemental than reason — something that civilized man has almost lost.

"But were you never lost at all?" someone once asked him.

"No, but one time for about half a day I was con-siderably bothered."

Over the miles and miles and miles of unending tree growth of the world of his young manhood, the squir-rels appeared to be as numberless as the ducks and geese that in winter came down in clouds and fed in constantly shifting rolls. "The thundercloud of pigeons blotting the sun" gave no sign of their coming extinction. In mating season, the yelp of the wild turkey could be heard in every direction, and the bellowing of alligators vibrated willow leaves hanging over the waters. Wild razorback hogs, so lanky for running and so tusked for fighting that they were a match for pork-hungry bears, had their refuges in the canebrakes and other dense growth; so did the bears and panthers. Alone with ax, knife and rifle, Ben Lilly would go into the swamps and cut his way to the most densely defended lair.

Around lakes and ponds and along bayous, colonies of nesting egrets whitened the trees. Before the end of the century the thoughtless vanity of American women in their demand for egret plumes to adorn hats and the heartless greed of hunters and traders almost exterminated these beautiful birds. The plumes, growing from a patch of the back, come to perfection only in the mating season. Waiting till the rookeries were "ripe" — until the eggs were hatched and the parent birds were staying by the nests — plume hunters would assault them with shotguns, killing them by the thousands, hauling the dead out of the waters in skiffs, getting as high as eighty dollars an ounce for the plumes. Ben Lilly never plume-hunted.

Overflow deposits of silt had for ages been creating

a soil as rich as ever fruited. Here the rainfall is abundant. Forests of red gum and white oak and giant cy-
presses edging the network of waters stood loftier than
almost any other trees east of the redwoods of the
Sierras. Black walnuts grew along with hackberries,
thorned honey locusts, tupelos, pecans, ash, and many
other trees. In places underbrush covered the ground;
in other places, palmettos. Canebrakes stretched for
miles and miles, the hollow stalks that waved their
green blades fifteen or twenty feet up in the air rooted
so densely that only bears, razorback hogs and a man
with a knife could penetrate them. These canebrakes
were the last refuge for hunted things, including some
men. A chaos of fallen timber — some trees prostrated
by decay, others felled by hurricanes — rank briars
and vines growing around, over, under and between the littered trunks and limbs, made barriers
impenetrable to any man who could not hack,
climb, and crawl. Stretches of prairie grew tall
grasses, and on them deer as well as domesticated
stock grazed.

There is no evidence that Ben Lilly ever read Audubon or was stimulated by him, but, like Audubon in
the woods of Louisiana, he found that "there is nothing perfect but primitiveness." To many people along
the primitive lowlands, however, the deadly timber

rattler and the cottonmouth moccasin were imperfections, and for months during every year swarms of malaria-carrying mosquitoes made the lives of human beings and of domestic stock miserable. According to a common saying, a variant from that applied to other places, Louisiana was all right for women (who slept indoors under mosquito bars) and for cats (protected by fur) but was hell on dogs and men. In Ben Lilly's youth, the mosquito country had many young widows whose husbands had died of malaria. Even he had it once, but he seemed generally immune to mosquitoes, ticks, redbugs and other insects. "The mosquitoes just go *ping* against my hide," he said, "but they can't make a dent." The only injury the land gave him was deafness in one ear, supposed to have been induced by too much sleeping on wet ground. He never had a cold, never "felt puny." His tonic was a tumbler of sweetened water.

The individualism of the inhabitants scattered through the woods tended to odd behavior rather than to unorthodox thinking. Original intellectual processes are not a part of the "rugged individualism" of the American tradition. There was the justice of peace, Will Kelly, for instance. He and his wife had eloped in Arkansas at the age of eighteen and settled on a farm on the Louisiana-Arkansas line. As he told the story, "I was poor and didn't have no money, but my niggers was always pestering me for two-and-a-half to buy marriage licenses with. So I sets down one day and writes myself a letter authorizing me to marry folks. I signs Governor Murphy J. Foster's name to it. Then I gets me a lot of Sears Roebuck order blanks. Then I performs the ceremony." A part of the ceremony consisted of a long recitation embodying:

Dark was the night, stormy was the weather;
Allow me to hitch this rogue and wench together.

"I'd charge the couple five dollars," Will Kelly proudly confessed, "to be paid after cotton-picking time the next fall, and, by grabs, I always collected. None of 'em ever got a divorce neither."

Young Lilly depended upon his farm for a livelihood, but he had no instinct for drudgery or for managing, no ambition to establish an estate. Once Billy Reneau found him furrowing with his horses at full gallop while he galloped behind them, holding the plow handles. One summer after a break in the Mississippi River brought water right up to his field fence, he repeatedly left his plow to leap the fence and wade into the slough waist deep to drink. Not unlike neighboring farmers, he let his stock, running out on the unfenced range, root-hog or die. The walls of his barn were ornamented with his paintings of cows, horses, alligators and other animals.

Near the barn was a blacksmith shop where he occasionally did work for other people as well as for himself. He preferred making knives to sharpening plow points.

> The smith, a mighty man was he,
> With large and sinewy hands.

He had "a hand like a ham." His strength became the pride and the wonder of the land, and he rejoiced to display it as a strong man rejoiceth to run a race. He would seize the hundred-pound blacksmith anvil by the snout, or horn, with one hand, lift it straight out and up, and then take both hands and toss it over his shoulder. In town, natives would lead him to the blacksmith shop to do the anvil feat. One day, after spectators had gathered, he grasped the anvil to lift it but could not. He seemed to be out of condition. He gripped the anvil horn so hard that blood burst out of his finger-ends.

His uncle had put up a big cotton gin, operated by horse power. Ben preferred air softened by the gossamer tufts from cottonwood trees to the floating lint that irritated all nostrils and lungs about the gin during cotton season. It is claimed that he could sink a pair of cotton hooks into a five-hundred-pound bale of cotton, hoist it to his back, and walk off with it.

In the prime of his life he weighed around one hundred and eighty pounds and was all sinew. He stood about five feet, nine inches or better, but the compacted vitality in his body made him look larger than he really was. He was barrel-chested, built like a panther. His wide shoulders, deep chest and narrow hips made him appear "as if the Creator had used a funnel or a top to pattern him by." On horseback the inherent energy and power of his frame seemed to dwarf the animal under him.

He was as lithe and active as he was strong and was the "champeen" athlete as well as hunter of the whole country. From sheer vigor and suppleness he ran and leaped as spontaneously as a fawn. The town marshal of Mer Rouge saw him jump flat-footed, from a standing position, 10 feet and 6 inches. Twenty-one years after his first marriage he was amusing his children by jumping. Out in the yard one December day in 1901, he took a brick in each hand and made three consecutive jumps. His deeply imprinted tracks became the subject of talk. On Christmas day some town people speculating on the distance measured the tracks with a tape. According to their memory, the three jumps covered 36 feet; the American record for the standing

[30]

A picnic crowd was paralyzed at a runaway horse hitched to a buggy carrying a helpless woman. Ben Lilly "leaped over the heads of people in his way" and overtook the flying horse. When he was fifty-six years old, in New Mexico, Ed Steele saw him head off some wild horses that ran past a corral gate. Specialists in charge of modern army training hold that running is more effective than all kinds of setting up exercises in giving young men endurance, muscle and agility.

Having been born and brought up "where frogs holler" and having, apparently, no more distaste for wetness than a duck, Ben Lilly, nevertheless, could not swim. Yet he had no fear of deep water and he could dive like an otter. If while on horseback he came to a river, he would either swim the animal across or dismount, head him into the water and swing on to his tail. If afoot, he would walk on the bottom — provided it was not too wide; he was very long-winded. Unless the water was very deep, he could hold his gun aloft. Perhaps he did not always keep it dry. No matter how he held it, the weight would ballast him and make underwater walking easier. L. L. Davidson saw him shoot a buffalo fish, jump into water up to his neck and get the fish out. He cared no more for fishing than for hunting rabbits. If cattle he was driving got into a mill in midstream, clambering over each other, so that animals inside the tightening circle were in danger of drowning, Lilly would rush among them, start one out for the bank, and hold on to it somehow, the other cattle following.

In the fall of 1880, despite a warning that "she's crazy," he married. Marriage did not improve her mental health. The hunts became more extended. Ben Lilly never did like roads. When the notion to hunt struck him, he might take out either afoot or on horse with his dogs and hunt for fifty or seventy-five miles before reversing his course. He established a movable camp in the woods, with black Tutt Alford to cook for the dogs. He had as many as twenty-five at one time, fed them corn bread, coon meat, bear meat, venison. He gave his wife credit for feeding the dogs well when they were at home.

He killed so many ducks one winter that she issued an order against bringing another one into the kitchen. He always rigged his own saddles, buying the trees; he rigged one with bearskin. He never took care of a saddle, and one day he aroused so much indignation by throwing his muddy saddle on the porch that he straightway resaddled and rode off again. When he came home wet and muddy himself, he would not change clothes. "It's better for the health to let them dry on you," he said. Once when he brought a friend in for dinner, they were served an old mud-covered boar's head that he had put in the smokehouse for the dogs. "It's good enough for you," his wife said as she slammed it, unwashed and half-cooked, on the table.

One day she said to him, "Ben, you like to shoot so well, why don't you get your gun and shoot that chicken hawk?"

"All right" — and Ben took his gun. The hawk flew. Ben followed. More than a year passed before he re-entered the house.

"That hawk kept flying," he remarked.

He had been over in the great Sunflower Swamp, seventy by thirty miles in area, on the Sunflower River in Mississippi. Before establishing camp in that wilderness, he spent three weeks exploring — without seeing a human face or hearing a blowing horn. This was about 1884. According to Buck Centers, he killed sixty-five bears in the Sunflower Swamp. He sold both the meat and the grease. He had a saddle rigged with block and line so that he could alone load the heaviest bear on a pack horse, trained to follow him.

It was on the Sunflower that he had the narrowest escape of his life from a black bear. He found where a very large male bear had been eating plums and he laid for him in the thicket. The bear came according to expectation, in the moonlight; Lilly shot and knocked him down. Thinking he had killed him, he leaned his gun against a tree and rushed to stab. Just as he raised his knife, the bear rose, with a powerful slap knocked the knife from his hand, and came on. Lilly ran around the nearest tree, the bear hot behind him. Around and around they went, the bear now and then nipping his hips. Ben Lilly afterwards said that he was nearer exhaustion than he had ever been in his life when, still moving, he almost stumbled on the bear in front of him — dead. After that he was cautious about laying aside his gun.

What drew him back home now and then was a frail child named Vernon and called Dick. One day a messenger found Lilly delivering a herd of cattle in Lake Providence. On the ride home he ruined a good horse, but little Dick was dead. He kneeled on the floor by the fragile form and his shoulders shook. His wife entered the room without his being aware of her presence. She looked at him a long time in silence, then laid a hand on his shoulder and said, "Why can't we live in harmony?" His shoulders stopped shaking. He stood up and said, "Lelia, the only tie between us is gone. Now, you go your way and I will go mine." He gave her "a roll of bills that would have choked a cow." Her way was to another marriage and then to thirty years in an insane asylum. For about a year after the child's death, Ben Lilly spent much of his time cutting bee trees in remote woods, selling the honey.

He had never cared in the least for farming. Not only did it interfere with hunting, but chickens, pigs, milk cows, crops, all bind a farmer to a domesticated plot of ground. Ben Lilly resented all bindings. He had worked into cattle trading before his divorce. Buying cattle and driving them to market took a man out. As a rule, he did not grow cattle, but animals he had bought were often scattered over the country. He was consistently determined not to be owned by any form of property. "Things" may "ride mankind." They were never to ride Ben Lilly. He could hunt between trades and space the trades as he pleased. By 1887 he was selling pieces of farm land to pay off debts. People said he "shot it up."

In 1890 he married again and by this union had three children, two daughters still living and a son who died of tuberculosis after he was grown. For his family he bought a place on the edge of the town of Mer Rouge, but came to it from the woods only once in a while to patch up a packsaddle or something like that. No "hostages to fortune" for him.

He did not have to have dogs to hunt. He might be riding along dogless, with a boy helper, on his way to buy a bunch of cattle, and suddenly say, "You go back. I need to go hunting." Perhaps a track across the road had decided him, perhaps a whiff of a current of air, perhaps a woods sound that stirred recollections. He would disappear, be gone two days, two weeks, two months.

In his brown duck trousers, heavy work shoes — never boots — and Boy Scoutish beaver hat, he was always ready to take any fork or any trail. He was not hampered by a toilet kit; he never shaved, though he usually kept his beard and hair groomed. Often piling into bed with his clothes on, even under a roof, he wanted no nightshirt for out-of-doors sleeping. The provisions he habitually carried were easily replenished — fresh corn in season and dry corn out of season. The dry corn might be on cobs or shelled and carried in a shot pouch. Sometimes he would parch the grains, sometimes eat them raw. There are many anecdotes of visiting hunters surprised at finding nothing but a few ears of corn in his camp. He had wonderful teeth.

If he had given his word to a man to be at a certain place at a certain time, he would be there. His dates were not so numerous that he needed a calendar to remind him of them. Often he gave his word to the creatures in the woods; he kept that word also. Settlers out in the sticks liked to deal with him so well that they would save their yearlings for him at three dollars a head rather than sell to someone else for a dollar more. For one thing, "Whatever Ben Lilly said was just that." Riding up to a planter's house, he would say, "I'm not out to buy your cattle. I want you to give them to me." He sold as easily as he bought. Sometimes in his trades he was "a curiosity of a man."

One afternoon, for instance, a man came to his place wanting to buy a milk cow. He was emphatic in requiring that the cow be perfectly gentle and capable of giving four gallons of milk a day. Ben Lilly had an extra good milk cow, he said, that he would sell for seventy-five dollars, calf thrown in. It was close to milking time. He hunted up four "pickaninnies," set them like clothespins on the cow's back, got his buckets, and while the cow chewed her cud, milked two measured gallons from her teats. The deal was closed.

He drove some cattle to Vicksburg, but usually sold to E. J. Hamley at Lake Providence, Louisiana. One time after he had delivered a drove to Hamley and was on his way home, he met Pete Vinson with a drove. He made Vinson a quick offer. Vinson accepted. "You deliver the cattle to Hamley for me," Lilly said. "I'll give you an order on him for the money. There's a bear waiting for me." Neither had a piece of paper to write on. They were stopped where timber cutters had recently been working. B. V. Lilly picked up a chip, smoothed it down with his knife, cut into it the amount of money to be paid Vinson and below the figures carved a honey bee and a water lily. "Just give this to Mr. Hamley," he said. Vinson said later that he "felt like a fool" presenting a chip of wood to a man, but Hamley was not surprised and paid over the money. Ben Lilly enjoyed rebuses. One time a letter with his return address on the envelope and pictures of a billy goat and a bunch of flowers, directed to Bonita, Louisiana, came to the postmaster at that place. He delivered the letter to Billy Flowers.

If Ben Lilly's ox got in the ditch on Sunday, it had to flounder there till Monday. After he had hunted a certain cow in the bottoms for two weeks, he was staying at a friend's house over Sunday. During the day the cow came up to the "stomp" in front of the house. Lilly would not open a gate to allow her to enter a little pasture, and he stood against anybody else's violating the Sabbath by opening the gate. Monday he started hunting the cow again but never got another glimpse of her.

Colonel Zack Miller of the 101 Ranch in Oklahoma told me that one spring he employed Lilly by the day to buy steers for him in Louisiana, contracting for delivery at a holding place near the railroad. After Lilly had been working about a month, Miller told him on a Saturday that they would load a train of steers the next day.

"Then you can pay me off," Lilly said.

"Why?"

"I don't believe in working on Sunday."

"You needn't work," Colonel Zack conceded. "You just rest in camp. There'll be plenty of hands to put the steers on the cars."

"I don't want to work for a man who works on Sunday," Lilly concluded. He had quit.

One Saturday evening he put a bunch of cattle in a "lot" — a pen — to hold over Sunday. They were thirsty. That night they made a run and broke out. Instead of going after them Sunday morning before they had time to scatter far, he would not saddle his horse or allow his hands to saddle until Monday came. He would not pay a hand off on Sunday. He did not pay a hand to work by the day, but by the day-and-night. That is an old cow-country custom.

During a hot summer spell while the moon was full, he was moving a bunch of about sixty gentle cattle. Cattle will not drive in excessive heat. The bunch was trailing along smoothly in the moonlight when Jep

Hughes, a boy helping drive them, heard Mr. Lilly yell, "Hold the cattle up!"

"Why?" Jep yelled back.

"It's midnight. Sunday has started. I forgot about that till just now."

"Well, it's not more'n four miles to Henry Jackson's pen."

"You know I never work on Sunday."

The cattle were no trouble to stop, and they soon bedded down on the open ground.

"I'm hungry," Jep said.

"Build a fire and roast that," and Ben Lilly handed out an ear of corn.

Jep rode on to food and a bed. Lilly stayed with the cattle and his ear of corn. Usually, if he were driving cattle on a week end he looked ahead and made it to some friend's house and pens. He did not handle big herds of cattle, only bunches of from fifty to two hundred head each. The country he drove over was so settled that he could pen every night and eat at houses.

If a hired boy on a drive asked him if he were hungry, he would say, "Why, no. If I was hungry, I'd eat some of these bushes. Look how the cattle do." Then he would break off a branch and chew it, pretending to relish it. "You can trot your horse as fast as you want to after cattle," he would tell a boy, "but you mustn't lope. Loping scares cattle." He knew that few boys will stand very long the rough jolting of a trot. He had a rule that if a boy let a cow brute get away, he must dismount and turn his horse loose with the herd, keeping up the drags on foot.

He could rope by head or foot, but roping was not one of his accomplishments. As a boy, R. W. Oldham saw him chase a wild steer a long time before getting close enough to rope it. Then the steer jumped a rail fence and jerked Lilly's horse over it. Lilly got off. The horse, a big brown named West, untrained to hold a rope pulling on the horn of a saddle, was helpless against the lunges of the steer. Lilly caught the bridle, close up, but got his finger hung so that the frantically plunging horse jerked him down and was dragging him. He managed with his free hand to reach the rifle he habitually carried in a scabbard slung to his saddle, pulled it out and shot the horse.

He knew how to tail — ride up against a bolting steer, grab his tail and jerk him off balance, making him swap ends. After a powerful tail-busting, the most stubborn brute usually heads back into the herd, his ambition to get away thoroughly cooled. Handling tough range cattle has never been a delicate business anywhere. Ben Lilly did not mind chopping off the horns of a fighting cow with an ax. A brute that he was once after wheeled to fight, stood trembling with rage between two saplings. Lilly leaped from his horse, mugged the animal to the ground, and while he held it down punched holes through its eyelids and sewed them together with laces pulled out of his shoes. A blinded cow brute will follow close behind other cattle, will not try to break away.

For a time Lilly rode a very strong, savage-natured stallion that he had to be wary of. One hot day after he had ridden the stallion unmercifully, he dismounted to drink from a clear pool of water. After drinking, he pulled on the rope tied around the stallion's neck to bring him down to the water. The stallion had gone mad, locoed from the heat. He made for his rider, knocked him down and was pawing him, but — active as a cat — Lilly reached the saddle gun, and killed the horse right there.

The one horse he is remembered as caring for was an excellent cow pony and hunting animal named Boone — after Daniel Boone. Lilly said that a pair of "Texas spurs" and an "ellum club" were responsible for the horse's training. Boone would drive cattle without a rider. If some wild cow Lilly was following entered a boggy morass impassable to the horse, he would dismount, fix the bridle reins over the saddle horn and tell Boone to go home. Boone went. The sight of

Ben Lilly's horse, saddled and riderless, was no sign for uneasiness.

Lilly had Boone on his hunt with Theodore Roosevelt. One day, a newspaper reporter chronicled, Lilly "got separated" from hunters accompanying him. In other words, they could not keep up with him. They made their way out of a canebrake back to camp. It was a dark rainy night. One hunter, a stranger in the country, suggested they fire guns to let Lilly know where camp was. "He'll come when he wants to," hunters who knew him said. At daybreak he trudged up, wet and muddy from a night after a bear. "Why, Ben, where's your horse?" one wanted to know. "Oh, he's down in the woods." Ben Lilly gave "a very shrill and peculiar call," and in about half an hour his cow pony, bridled and saddled, came up.

Not Ben Lilly's was the Western philosophy that "a man on foot is no man at all." He would ride a horse hunting until the going got too hard except for a footman or the trail too interesting for him to remain off the ground. Then he would quit his horse, perhaps leaving it tied with a string so that if he did not get back within a day or two it could break away and go to feed and water. Sometimes he staked the horse — and would not get back to the suffering animal for a week.

In reminiscing, he never referred to a horse. At best a horse was to him an agent to accomplish something desired, not something desirable in itself. Had he savored the feelings of animation and power that a good horse imparts to a congenial rider, Ben Lilly would not, when he got to the big ranching country, have become more of a footman than ever — and thus more of an oddity. For some years after his arrival in the West, he used burros to move camp headquarters. He might ride one from camp into the mountains as far as any hoofed quadruped could go and then turn it loose to make its own way back. The more he hunted, the less use he had for even a burro.

A horse makes noise, warning all hearing things of his approach. A horse's size makes him highly visible. In woods or brush, in mountains or in lowlands, a soft-stepping man, stooping here, keeping cover there, sees under and through trees and bushes, whereas on horseback he looks only against them. From a horse's back a man sees tracks and other signs afar off; on the ground, he sees them as if with a magnifying glass. The spur-wearers who ride with hounds dismount to scrutinize the ground when the trail grows baffling. Ben Lilly stayed in a position to scrutinize the ground. As he freed himself from farm and family because they require that a man turn back to them, he freed himself from horses. He chose to be free to hunt on and on, pulled by something beyond the exhilaration of fleet movement and brave sounds traditionally associated with the chase.

He surpassed all other men in making, and was noted for, three kinds of sounds: horn-blowing, cow-calling and whip-popping. He made his own blowing horns, carving figures of bears, panthers, bucks and dogs on them. His horn notes carried far and musical like the voice of Bugle Ann. He could blow tunes on his horn. According to the code of the horn-blowers, three blasts meant, "Come to me. Answer"; two blasts meant, "Where are you?" and one blast announced, "Here I am."

In Louisiana the old custom of calling cattle to feed and salt is still kept up. If they will come to the call, calling them is a much easier way of gathering them out of the woods than hunting them down. If they come a few times, however, and find no salt, no Spanish moss cut down from the trees or other food to reward them, they grow indifferent to the calling. The orthodox call starts out as if the Rebel yell were on the way and ends with a kind of cooing. Ben Lilly, it is claimed, could *Hi-ee-oo* so loud and clear that on a still day cows and people three miles away heard him. His call was such that a cow a long way off would sometimes answer with a *moo* as she started toward its source.

The talk of the country, however, was Ben Lilly's cowwhip. In cow work it was his chief dependence, for both bark and bite. Individuals recalling it differ radically as to its length; it was certainly eighteen feet long and, counting the long snapper, or popper, it may have tapered out to thirty feet. It was made of eight strands of rawhide that Lilly himself had artfully plaited around a core of grass rope. An inch or more thick at the base, it tapered to a fine point, to which the popper was attached. A whip's popper wears out quickly, and Lilly always carried a "sea grass" (manila or sisal hemp) rope around his waist or buckskin thongs in a pocket to make poppers from. The whip handle was an eighteen-inch piece of hickory, polished from much handling. The whip and handle were so heavy that a boy who tried to pop it — and the ambition of every boy was to pop it — could hardly swing the popper from the ground. One Lilly whip placed on the scales weighed, it is claimed, twenty-two-and-a-half pounds.

He did not swing the whip, but used a wrist and elbow movement, forward, backward and then forward, not only to pop it but to cut it into the flesh of whatever he willed to exert his power over. In early days the skill of a bullwhacker freighting west of the Missouri River was tested by his ability to fleck a fly with his whip cracker off an ox twenty or thirty feet away without disturbing a hair of the ox. No bullwhacker was ever more accurate and skillful with whip than Ben Lilly. He would bet ten dollars that he could pop the loosened tops off ten beer bottles without turning over a bottle. It was a sure bet with him, but he never collected a cent, for he would no more wager for keeps than he would hunt on Sunday. He could pop the tune of "Yankee Doodle" with his whip. He could pop a grapevine as a makeshift whip.

The air-shattering report of his popper would make a cow jump out of her skin. If the sound did not make her move, he might knock her down with a terrific lash across her back. In woods that prevented maneuvering the whip in the air, he could bring it up under an animal's belly strong enough to slash the hide. Sometimes a cow brute will "sull" — become so hot and maddened that it will not move. If such an animal was not sulking to the point of death, Ben Lilly's whip would budge it. It made many a stubborn cow, steer or bull bellow with pain. He would not allow any of his hands to carry a whip. L. L. Davidson was riding along the road with him one day when a dog dashed out fiercely from a Negro cabin. This dog had scared his cattle on other occasions and he had warned the owner. Now, with the rapidity of a gunman pulling his six-shooter, he cut down on the dog and whipped it to death.

One time out on a country road, Lilly rode up behind a Dr. Callaway mounted on a spirited horse, of which he was afraid and which he was holding in with one hand while he grasped the horn of his saddle with the other. Ben Lilly gave the horse a cut with his long whip, and after that the doctor had to use both hands to hold on while the horse burned the breeze. The race ended at the end of the road, where the doctor's patient lived. He burst in calling for a gun with which to kill his tormentor. The people, Lilly's friends, calmed him down. "After that he was not afraid of his horse any more."

That Hawk Kept Flying

WILD Bill Hickok, the story goes, shooting only a derringer pistol, cut a rooster's throat at thirty yards without breaking its neck. In a delightful essay entitled "Folklore Shooting," * Frost Woodhull remarks that no derringer cartridge was ever "capable of such accuracy even in a fine rifle barrel, much less in a miserable little popgun. Merely wrapping Wild Bill's fist around a derringer would not make a target gun out of it." One of Billy the Kid's admirers used to tell how he had seen the Kid empty a Colt forty-one six-shooter at snowbirds darting past him in the air and, one by one, cut off six heads. Whoever credits this story simply does not know the ballistic facts of the Colt forty-one.

Any man who does anything better than other people can do it is sure to have detractors; he is equally sure to have magnifiers. One story goes that Ben Lilly

* Published by the Texas Folklore Society, Austin, Texas, in *Southwestern Lore* (*Publications* No. IX), 1931.

perfected the fine points of his marksmanship by shooting mosquitoes with a .22-caliber rifle. Those mosquitoes were probably of the breed that stuck their proboscises into the iron washpot covering little Pecos Bill and flew off with it. Yet no one can prove that Ben Lilly did not shoot mosquitoes with his .32 rimfire rifle. He shot, on the wing, not only bats but bumblebees and yellow jackets; he made targets of even the lovely "dolly birds," a local name for cedar waxwings. He brought down circling buzzards from high in the air, knocking feathers out of their falling bodies with each repeated shot. One day while he was walking over a field with Bob Causey, a duck flew up near them. "Watch me shoot that duck's bill off, Bob," he said. A bullet had cut the bill off before the sentence was finished. With a bullet he could cut a small branch under a leaping squirrel and then riddle the squirrel with lead before it hit the ground. This at a distance of "maybe a city block" — or maybe of only a fifty-foot lot. He had extraordinary eyes for what he was interested in seeing. Once he located a bear by noticing a gentle motion of tree leaves near the opening of a hollow limb. The breathing of a bear inside the hollow stirred the leaves. On the other hand, his eye for deer was mediocre. He was not interested in deer.

One time Jim Kelly, desiring meat, offered to

furnish ammunition to Ben Lilly for killing squirrels. The two went out together. Before long twenty-five squirrels were in the sack — and Lilly was using up more ammunition than ever. Kelly saw that he was making a sieve out of every squirrel as it fell, putting five or six holes through some of them. If Lilly wanted a squirrel to eat, himself, he would often jar the limb under it with a heavy bullet and bring it down untouched. The one time he is known willfully to have shot on Sunday was at a squirrel. He was resting in camp. Two men with him were shooting at and missing a squirrel in a tree about a hundred yards off. Finally Ben Lilly grabbed his rifle, leveled it and with one shot extinguished the target.

As a buck "sharpens" his horns by hooking a bush, Lilly made his aim for big animals more deadly by practicing on small ones. In his lack of sensitivity towards wild things he was, during his more ebullient years at least, a brutal exterminator. Except for one lone bear, he exterminated all bears from a wide area in Louisiana, and he greatly reduced them in other areas. One day he shot eleven deer alongside the road while going two miles from his farm to a neighbor's. Like his great predecessor of the Louisiana woods, John James Audubon, he destroyed what he sought. Audubon said: "I call birds few when I shoot less than one hundred per day." "I was in the woods, the woods of Louisiana, my heart was beating with joy," Audubon cried. At this time he was painting the best known of all his bird pictures, the picture of the lordly wild turkey gobbler; in one day of this time, he helped kill twenty alligators, "these beautiful creatures," as he called them.

Ben Lilly did not practice exclusively on live flesh. He would, it is said, fasten a corncob so that it lay lengthwise to him, step off some distance, and drill the pith out of it with a small-caliber bullet. It is doubtful if there has ever been a better marksman among the hunters of America, but he could not demonstrate that marksmanship in public.

Once he was talked into entering an exhibition of trapshooting clay pigeons with a pump shotgun. The spectators and the waiting so excited him that he missed the pigeon the first shot. But then, pumping like greased lightning, he not only broke the clay but successively shattered the broken parts. In shooting, as in everything else, he was himself only in solitudes, though a fellow hunter or two did not bother him. It was not that he shunned publicity. Many of his acts appear to have been designed to make himself conspicuous. He had the instincts but lacked the brass of a showman. If placed on a stand to await game driven by dogs or men, he grew too nervous to hit it when it appeared. He was good at chasing game by stands for others, but taking a stand was not his idea of hunting.

Anything that jumped up suddenly within range of his eye and gun had as well be marked off. One day while he was calling cows in Louisiana with a man named Davenport, he spied a buck standing in a thicket watching them. He had no gun and it was a mile to one. He told Davenport to stay where he was and to keep on calling cows. He rode for a gun, came back, slipped into position for shooting the curious buck still standing. Preparation had made Lilly too eager. He fired and almost missed, giving the animal only a slight flesh wound; but when it leaped he killed it.

Though he hunted birds occasionally in Louisiana, he had little use for a shotgun. His preferred way of killing ducks was with a rifle. He shot their heads off. One time he sent to his home a whole barrel of ducks, every one of them beheaded — and all spoiled before they arrived. He could call wild turkeys with his mouth and he had no use for a caller of bone or wood. From responses made by turkeys, he knew whether they were going or coming. One time he called up three gobblers for his friend L. L. Davidson to shoot. They had come to within about eighty yards when a saddle horse, hidden back in the brush, snorted. The gobblers broke to run in the opposite direction. Lilly pointed his rifle and killed all three quicker than you can say "Jack Robinson." Then he apologized to Davidson for killing them, saying they were out of shotgun range. On a wild hog hunt he and a visiting sportsman agreed to see which could shoot the most hogs rounded up by dogs in a clump of swampy growth. They took stands on opposite sides of it. Lilly killed all eighteen hogs in the bunch before the other man got a chance to fire. He began on the hog nearest to his opponent and anticipated him on every shot.

He claimed that he never missed anything that he shot at, provided nothing went wrong with his gun and he was on his own grounds. In 1928, he wrote an old friend in Louisiana: "I am sure I improve in shooting all the time. If a bear or lion ever jumps out of a tree and I am in sight, I will get three balls in it before it hits the ground. I never saw a lion that I did not kill or wound. I shoot well at ranges up to 400 yards, running or standing, with a .30–30 or .33 or .303-caliber. At long range I kill by holding the sight high over the animal." Men who are good at anything know that they are good.

The reputation of Ben Lilly as a marksman depends

on the testimony of others, not on his own few allusions to the subject. While a Biological Survey trapper was hunting with him in an Arizona canyon, Lilly's dogs put a panther on a narrow inaccessible ledge, out of view of the hunters. The trapper climbed with great difficulty to a position whence he could see the lion. Just as he glimpsed it, it was preparing to leap. He yelled to Lilly. The lion sailed off and down towards the dogs. Before it got to them, it was dead with three bullets through vital spots.

Ben Lilly had no use for braggarts. A Louisiana hunter started boasting to him about the bears he had killed. At first Lilly was interested in swapping experiences, but he soon noticed that every time he told about killing a bear the man would tell about killing a bigger one under more exciting conditions. Presently he went to his house and brought back a pair of very large alligator tushes and, without saying a word, held them out for inspection. The man said, "That must have been a pretty fair-sized bear." Lilly walked away in disgust. Alligator teeth are not fitted into jaw sockets like those of a bear; they are hollow and grow over a bony structure. Any hunter of experience knows the difference.

Late in life Ben Lilly told Frank Rives that he had fired a pistol only once. He said that one afternoon out in Arizona he came upon two prospectors shooting with a .45 Colt at the Ace of Spades card tacked up against a tree. One of the prospectors handed him the six-shooter. He leveled down, pulled the trigger, knocked out the black spot, and returned the gun.

Ben Lilly belonged to the fighting South at a time when knives and fists as well as pistols were commonly used to settle private "difficulties" — and difficulties were exceedingly common. The reputation of the West for killers has been glorified, but there were actually more killings in the Old South than in the West. The Western code of violence was derived from the South. The West specialized in six-shooters; the South in knives. The early Virginians were known as "Big Knives." Probably the most violent section of America, excepting transient mining camps and boom towns, was the Louisiana-Mississippi-Arkansas country of Lilly's youth and the generation immediately preceding.

Towards the end of the first quarter of the nineteenth century, Jim Bowie, who was famous for his use of cold steel in Louisiana before he came to Texas to die in the Alamo, and other Southerners made the knife that took Bowie's name the bloodiest instrument ever utilized in American bloodletting. In anger a man of the bayou country would yell, "I'll wash my knife in the blood of your God-damn heart." Morehouse Parish, Lilly's home, was where the most desperate and notorious of all Mississippi River thugs, John Murrell, leader of the far-spread Murrell gang, was hanged. This Murrell often killed slaves he had stolen. One time, the story goes, he was hurrying a bunch of stolen blacks through the woods when one of them, a young pregnant woman, kept falling behind. "Why don't you keep up?" he yelled to her. "Because of my burden." "Then I'll take the burden out of you" — and Murrell slashed his "Arkansas toothpick" deep across the woman's abdomen, leaving her to bleed to death.

Bowie-knife culture was a part of Ben Lilly's inheritance; yet it seems to have become no part of him. He made and used the "Lilly knife." The farms and plantations that he knew as a young man and the big ranches that he hunted over as an old man generally had blacksmith shops; he never stayed long at any place with a blacksmith shop without puttering in it. He fashioned his knives out of old files, horseshoer's rasps, automobile springs, any usable steel at hand. He delighted in fashioning the tooth of a big rake into a paring knife to be presented to a woman.

A knife to be serviceable to him in Louisiana had to be big and strong enough to hew an opening through

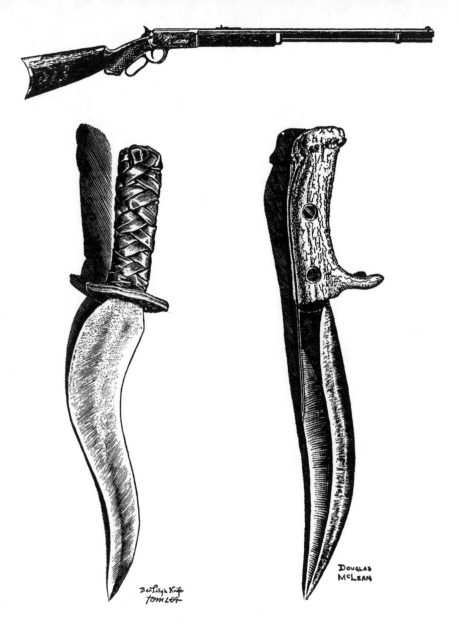

Ben Lilly's bear gun (drawn by Douglas McLean) and two of his famous Lilly knives. The knife at left, drawn by Tom Lea, is credited with having been stuck into 27 bears. Ben Lilly came from a line of steelsmiths; he made knives when he was a boy and was still making them in his dotage. His best knives were "tempered in panther oil."

a canebrake. The typical Lilly knife was always big enough to do the work of a Mexican machete; except for its curves and double edges, it was more like a butcher knife than a gentleman's hunting knife. Some of his blades were eccentrically shaped — in accordance with his own eccentricities. He wanted a knife, he said, that would gouge rather than plunge straight in. He wanted the blade sharp on both edges from tip to haft so that if he got it inside a bear it would cut in any direction he pulled or twisted it. He said he would rather have a blade break than bend. To temper the steel properly, he cooled it in bear or panther oil — preferably panther — and then gradually reheated it to the "drake-neck" color. He handled his blades with buckhorn. Hardly ever did he forge a metal guard on the knife. In addition to the big hunting knife, he generally carried a small skinning knife. The scabbards, like the knives, were his own handiwork.

He liked to give his knives to people he esteemed. To Tom Lea, Sr., of El Paso he gave a knife that he claimed to have stuck into twenty-seven bears. Some time after he had been hunting with Dr. A. K. Fisher, in the Black Range of New Mexico in 1918, he sent him a knife, razor-sharp on both edges, wrapped in paper from around a cracker box, on which was written: "This knife is made in camp in

People speculated on what he might do. Before long, while out hunting, he saw his false accuser riding pompously down a lane on a white horse. He ran through the woods to the lane fence, leaned his gun against a rail, crawled through to the road and stood there facing the rider.

"Mr. Blank," he said, "I'd like to speak to you."

"Very well, sir."

"You have accused me of stealing your cattle."

"Well, if you didn't, I don't know who did."

"Get down off that horse. I'm going to whip the clothes off you with the double of your own rope."

Lilly grasped the bridle reins of the horse. The rider begged like a baby, apologized, agreed to make a public withdrawal of his accusations. Lilly let him go.

Honesty was one of his lifelong prides. One time while hunting on Diamond Creek in New Mexico he came upon a spotted steer caught in a crevice and crippled beyond recovery. He butchered it for his famished dogs. Then he blazed a tree beside the Diamond Creek Trail and on the blaze penciled an explanation of his butchering the steer. He would no more have taken a piece of property belonging to another man than he would have paid a manicurist to trim his toenails.

His mildness was not of the kind that makes some

men doormats for the feet of others. One time his dogs badly mutilated a hog belonging to a Louisianian named Brewer. Brewer came to his camp with gun in hand and blood in his eye. "I'm going to kill your dogs," he said. "No," Lilly replied, "don't shoot my dogs. I'll pay you for the hog. You set the price." But Brewer was set on killing the dogs. "All right," concluded Lilly, picking up his gun, "you make the first shot and I'll make the second." Brewer left camp without shooting.

During his jumping days, Ben Lilly had fights, but all of them seem to have been in play. They were rough aplenty. One time he came up on a big youngster named Wid Harp bullying two boys.

"If you want to play, I'll play bear fight with you," he said to Wid.

"I don't know how to play bear fight," Wid replied.

"I'll show you," the agile Lilly went on. "I'll be the bear myself. I'll be down on my all fours trying to bite and cuff you. You fight me off with a stick the best way you can. You'd better get a good stick, because this is going to be a real bear fight."

Wid picked up the first chunk at hand, which turned out to be rotten. Lilly got down on his hands and knees, growled his deepest, and made a lunge. Wid's stick broke at the first blow. Lilly saw an opening

[64]

and went to biting ankles, mauling body and scratching face into a flitterjig. When he turned Wid loose, Wid was in a good humor but wanted to be the bear himself and play some more.

Lilly was entirely agreeable. He selected a stout club. At the first lunge, the bear got cracked over the head so hard that he was laid out cold, temporarily.

A "cow stomp" is a place where cattle congregate. It is always an open place. In low, wet land of the South where insects sometimes persecute livestock until they die, cattle find out and generation after generation repair to certain patches of ground comparatively free of mosquitoes and buffalo gnats — the chief insect persecutors. Perhaps some mineral inherent in these patches of ground emanates a vapor, or perhaps excretions from the cattle give the ground an odor repellent to the insects. Cattle come to these stomps to sleep, stand on them for hours in daytime. In the old days, men themselves sometimes took refuge on cattle stomps to get relief from mosquitoes.

One day, riding up to a stomp, Ben Lilly saw his friend Rufe Harp standing there, getting a respite from slapping at insects. Rufe Harp was a large and powerful man, and this day he seemed to be feeling playful. As Lilly got down off his horse to visit, he said, "Let's play bullfight." For half an hour the two butted head against head, bellowed, and pushed each other all over the stomp.

At another meeting these two started a "rooster fight." To play rooster, opponents cross forearms over chests and strike each other with elbows. A blow can be very painful to elbow as well as to other flesh and bone. As Ben Lilly and Rufe Harp roostered that day, they sounded like a pair of mules kicking each other.

This cock-and-bull play is an expression of animalism that also vents itself in practical joking. The joking may represent healthy animal spirits, but the amount of wit involved would entitle it to be called "oxplay" rather than "horseplay." George Meredith held that the civilization of a people is to be gauged by the amount of "thoughtful laughter" in their humor. The civilization of people whose humor lies mostly in practical jokes is as low as that typified by comic strips. Yet some wits have been practical jokers early in life. Mark Twain was a practical joker in a limited way until he suffered a fake holdup one night after he had been lecturing in a Nevada mining camp. Until the years matured him, Ben Lilly epitomized the whole tradition of rustic humor. At no time was he witty.

His most noted practical joke was on George Stivers, one of his hunting cronies and cow hands. One time he took Stivers out in a skiff amid woods overflowed by the Mississippi River. Miles away from dry land, he pretended to see a wild turkey in a tree farther on. He suggested that Stivers stand on a log while he himself rowed for a shot. Stivers got off on the log and lost sight of the rower almost immediately. The mosquitoes were fierce. After fighting them for hours, he saw Lilly rowing a few yards off and appearing not to see him. Stivers was too enraged and worn out to speak. After a little while, Lilly looked back, appeared to be surprised and called out, "Why, hello, George! What are you doing out here?"

Stivers went with Lilly on one other, and only one other, excursion — a winter hunt. A heavy snow fell on their camp, and, although Lilly disdained tents, he now crawled into the one Stivers had set up. Stivers was a heavy sleeper. About the time he got to snoring heartily, Lilly rolled him out into the snow, where he went on sleeping for a while, at least until Lilly had fallen asleep. When he awoke, nearly frozen, and perceived the trick, he poured a can of coal oil on the tent and set it afire. Lilly had to dive through fire to get out. Practical joking had been carried too far, he said.

As he rode up to Dock Harp's farm one day, he noticed a new homemade harrow near the gate. He pretended to be greatly frightened at it, snorted like a scared horse, jumped down, pulled his rifle from the scabbard, and, walking backward, riddled the harrow with bullets. He had had a narrow escape, he vowed, from a "new kind of fearful animal." Not many days after this episode, he returned, riding a new saddle. He had pulled it off his horse and was throwing it across the yard fence, when Dock came running out of the house with a shotgun. He filled the new saddle with buckshot. Ben Lilly told him that was "a childish thing to do."

Once he took two town hunters, eager to kill a bear, into the canebrakes, put them on separate stands, said he would chase the bear into view, and went back to town. All day in the rain they waited. . . . A Negro working for him wanted to headlight for coons. Lilly accommodated him, delegating a white man to come along with a gun. Before they had gone far in the darkness, Lilly separated from them — to "scout," he said. Then his accomplice fired at what he claimed was a pair of eyes. The next instant Lilly rushed forward on all fours, growling like a bear. The Negro was scared white.

Lilly stampeded a sleeping camp by the old ruse of hitching himself between the shafts of a rattletrap buggy and running with it over the bed ground, while a three-hundred-and-fifty-pound confederate named Big John Naff sat in the buggy lamming its sides with trace chains and yelling "whoa" at every breath. The scatterment of the sleepers was at its climax when Lilly suddenly sent buggy and Big John over a bank into ten feet of water. After Big John got back to land, it took all the men in camp to prevent him from killing his fellow joker.

One time while leading a herd of about one hundred and fifty cattle, Ben Lilly saw a circus caravan containing a loose camel and a loose elephant. The idea occurred to him that it would be great fun to stampede the circus animals. He rode back and with the help of his willing hands got his cattle headed in a long run for the caravan, but when those little "canebrake splitters" saw the elephant, they were the ones to stampede. It took a week to regather them.

There was no trouble to which he would not go to carry out his joke, and the torment to which it might subject man or beast concerned him little. His sole reservation to practical joking was that it be on a friend, and virtually all people who knew him were his friends. Camping with Lilly one night on a hunt, Mark Harp heard his horse groaning as if in great distress. He went under a tree, where the horse was, to investigate. He found that a rope had been tied to the horse's tail and pulled up over a limb so that the horse's hind feet were suspended off the ground. He said he never was able to figure out how Ben Lilly managed to hoist such a weight.

One night Lilly stopped at the Mark Harp farm on a cow-buying expedition with a boy helper named Cuba Causey who was ailing and who was sent to bed early. There were two beds in the room, and when Lilly and Tom Harp and his brother Bob got ready to turn in, Mr. Lilly said that, on account of being sick, Cuba had better be left to sleep alone. This was before the days of screening; most beds in the country had mosquito bars.

As Tom started to let down the mosquito bar, Mr. Lilly said, "No, don't do that. Leave the bar up so we can get more air. I'll keep the mosquitoes off you. Listen! I hear one now," and he slapped down on Tom's head with his big hand. "I got him. I'll sure keep 'em off you," he assured him.

"Every time I moved," Tom Harp recalls, "Mr. Lilly heard a mosquito and 'got him.' I lost account of the number he got. Finally, away after midnight, I thought that Mr. Lilly was asleep and very cautiously began to ease out of bed with the idea of crawling in under the bar with Cuba. Just as I got my legs out of bed and was about to straighten up, Mr. Lilly caught me by the shirt tail and yanked me back, saying, 'You mustn't bother Cuba. He's sick. I hear a mosquito now.' He mashed it on my head. He never missed that head. The mosquitoes and the floggings together finally exhausted me. While we were getting up the next morning, he said, 'Wasn't the mosquitoes b-a-a-a-d last night?' "

He was fond of all children, including his own. He never failed to greet a boy courteously, sometimes calling him "Podnah," showing interest in him, no matter how many men were around. He seemed to feel more at ease with boys than with rough men. "I was at the goslin' stage, all hands and feet and self-consciousness," Tom Harp remembers, "when one day in town I saw Mr. Lilly talking to a crowd of our local brass. I was drawn to him as iron filings are drawn to a magnet, but stopped on the outer edge of the circle. Presently he saw me, dropped the talk, came over, shook my hand, and asked me that old neighborly question, 'How are your maw and paw?' He did not get down on a boy's level but made a boy feel that he was a member of the human race."

"Everybody had a bed for Ben Lilly." He did not always sleep in it, however. As his old cowhand, Charlie McEalrath, says, "Ben, he was a notionous sort of a feller." One time he rode up to the Sammons place about dark, ate supper, and then declared he was going to sleep outside "in the waggin." At daylight he wasn't in sight. Just at breakfast time, he walked up from the slough carrying a big gobbler he had shot flying off the roost.

On approaching some friendly house, he would tootle a kind of tune on his hunting horn. The people would know that Ben Lilly was coming before they saw him. He might ride to the lot, unsaddle and feed his horse before presenting himself. Or he might halt at the yard gate, pick up a child and take him or her for a short ride before unsaddling. One time he rode up to a yard gate and called for a little girl that he was particularly fond of. After the mother came out and told him the child had died, he stood by the gate weeping for a while and then rode on. Often he modeled for children animal figures out of the clayey black gumbo. For a girl he might carve a folding fan; for a boy, a hunting horn. He would draw wild animal pictures for old and young alike. If children were around and he saw a horse pacing, he would beat time with his forefinger and chant:

> Twinkle, twinkle, little star,
> How I wonder what you are,
> Up above the world so high,
> Like a diamond in the sky.

Once he was settled, children crowded around him not only for candy but for stories. He needed little encouragement to tell of his encounters with bears, though there is no recollection of his making up tall tales or passing on any of the folk tales that have for generations been weaving around the animal that walks like a man. His hunting stories made him as welcome to any household where he stopped as was troubadour of old singing for his supper within the baron's castle walls.

Over and over for children he had to tell and was pleased to tell one story especially. To tell it here, I am patching together, using my own thread, details that eight or ten youthful listeners, now gray-headed, have remembered.

"Well, how about the time I crawled into a holler log and caught a bear by the hind legs and pulled him out?"

Universal approval.

"Or how about that bear I caught in a trap and rode with my spurs on while I was sticking him?"

"Yes, tell about riding a bear!"

"I might tell you about the time I climbed up a big dead tree trunk and went down into its holler for two cubs and the old mama bear came backing down after me."

"Yes, tell that, tell that."

[73]

"But I believe I'll tell you about another bear."

Momentary disappointment. The experienced ones among the children knew that before the visit was over they would get all the stories.

"Well, I was just rambling over by Forkid Oak Slough one morning and saw where a bear'd been eating corn out of my field. His trail was so plain I couldn't keep from follering it, even if I didn't have any dog to help me. After a while it got so fresh I thought sure I'd find him in some pin oaks just ahead. I walked under 'em and saw where he'd been up the biggest tree eating acorns and dropped out. Maybe he had smelled me.

"Yes, I've seen a bear away up in a tree roll himself into a ball and drop to the ground fifty or sixty feet. You'd think a fall like that would hurt a bear. I guess it don't. 'Course, an old gran'pa bear wouldn't drop very far maybe, but young active bears have limber bones, and when one of them rolls out of a tree it's about like a sleepy-headed boy rolling off the bed.

"Well, at this pin oak flat the trail got fresher than ever. The sun was way past noon now, and I ate an acorn or two myself. Next, the trail led into a cane-brake. I knew it wasn't too far acrost it. I went slow. The cane was so thick I had to cut it with my knife and make a hole to crawl through. I worked as quiet as a kitten sleeps. The wind was with me, so it wouldn't carry my smell to the bear.

"Then all of a sudden, I heard *whoof*, *whuff*, just like that. The next second a bear and me was all mixed up. There were two bears. They had come together in the canebrake. One ran off.

"The one that stayed was right on top of me. I couldn't shoot him, he was so close. He was as surprised as I was, but he didn't seem so anxious to part company. Not one black bear in ninety will fight, but this was the one. His tongue was as red as the wolf's when he showed it to Little Red Riding Hood. I didn't have time to ask him why his claws were so sharp. He was showing me how sharp they were without saying anything. The hole in the cane wasn't big enough to let me roll over, and there I was right under him."

"Did the old bear hug you?" Bob McGowen almost whispered.

"No, bears don't hug. They slap. The front paw is a club." And Mr. Lilly could not resist a gentle demonstration on his questioner.

Here, an excited ten-year-old screeched out, "But what did you do, Mr. Lilly? What did you do?"

"I just stuck my knife into his throat and worked it like churning butter. D'reckly he quit trying to get me. I drug him to a tree outside the canebrake and hung him up and went on.

"The bear that had run off bothered me. His tracks told me he was the one I had started out follering that morning. I was more anxious to meet him than ever, and I kept on trailing. The sun was way down low now. It was getting darkish under the big trees. Then I heard one of them old ivory-billed lord-gods cry, and looked up just in time to see the red on top of his head. This big woodpecker was flying away from a cypress tree that stood up higher than any other tree along the edge of a bayou. The bear tracks were going straight to it. When I got closer, I saw that it was holler. I says to myself, 'Well, Mr. Bear thinks he'll play Hide and Seek.' He was to do the hiding and I was to do the seeking.

"Sure enough, the tracks went square against the tree, but I couldn't be sure whether he was inside the holler or away up on one of the branches. By now it was too dark for me to see very far, but I didn't have to make a test to find out if the bear was up there. I knew he was.

"You know how to test a bear tree? Well, you cut some green, limber pegs with your knife and drive them into the bark around the tree trunk. Then you go off. If the bear is not in the tree when you leave but goes up during the night, he will mash the pegs so that they bend upwards. If he is up there and comes down while you are gone, the pegs will point downwards.

"While I was standing by the bear tree, a big old owl went to asking me, 'Who-o, who-o, who-o?' And I says, 'Who, yourself?'

" 'Mr. Bear,' I calls up, 'I hope you have a comfortable bed for the night. Mine is smooth and nice and clean, I thank you.'

"Then I drank some water out of the bayou just six steps off and came right back to the holler cypress. I nearly always carry supper with me, and I pulled out an ear of corn and ate it slow, one grain at a time. *Chew, chew, chew.* I called up and asked Mr. Bear if he wouldn't like a little of the corn, but he didn't say anything. I left some grains on the cob anyhow so that if he didn't want it, I'd have breakfast.

"Then I lay down with my feet inside the holler and went to sleep."

"But, Mr. Lilly," one boy wanted to know, "wasn't you scared to go to sleep with that old bear up there?"

"Yes, and he could climb down on top of you and bite you before you waked up," a little girl chimed in.

"No, no," Mr. Lilly explained. "Didn't I tell you a bear always climbs down backward? If this one

[77]

climbed down outside the tree, I would hear him scratching the bark and shoot him. If he came down the holler, he'd have to back into my feet and I would kick him and make him go up again. Sure enough, I hadn't been asleep more'n two hours before I felt something touch my foot. I kicked and it was Mr. Bear. He climbed back up faster'n a squirrel scooting away from a dog. I slept sounder now, for I knew where the bear was and knew he couldn't jump down from the tree. Along in the night he backed into my feet again and got another kick.

"Well, when daylight come, I noticed Mr. Bear hadn't eaten the corn I left for him, and so I had breakfast. *Chew, chew, chew.* I stood off a ways from the tree and hollered to him to come down. I asked him which he'd ruther have, a knife or a bullet; but he wouldn't say anything. I looked up the holler, but it was as dark as the inside of a cow. I punched a long pole up there, but the holler seemed all empty.

"After the sun got up high enough to make the ground speckled, I walked off a good way to make Mr. Bear think I was leaving. I sung him a song, saying,

Good-by, Mr. Bear, good-by,
But better keep open one eye.

[78]

I had my gun ready. I picked out a place where I could look at the holler place and see away up the trunk too. And then, what you guess I saw? I saw Mr. Bear's head sticking out of a hole clear at the top almost, and looking at me. The hole wasn't big enough for his body to come through. His ears were pointed like he couldn't make out why I kept piddling around his house. 'Mr. Bear,' I says to him,

> 'You clumb mighty high,
> But I'll fetch you nigh.'

"I took aim and pulled the trigger. That head disappeared, and *ker-plop*, right down through the holler tree trunk and on to the ground where my feet spent the night, a dead bear came."

CHAPTER IV

Teddy Roosevelt's Chief Huntsman

LATE one evening during the memorable freeze of 1898–1899, Ben Lilly appeared afoot at the home of his friend Robert Parsons in northern Louisiana. He consumed a great supper, disregarding his theory that a man should eat one dish alone and not mix foods in his stomach. After supper by the warm fire, he told Parsons that he had left the trail of two panthers in the snow, a male and a female. He wanted Parsons to take up the chase with him early next morning.

"Those panthers," Parsons told him, "would have to have gold heads and gold tails to set me out after them at four o'clock in the morning in this weather."

Ben Lilly sat by the fire and glowed at the prospect. He had no dogs with him. Long before daylight next morning he disappeared. During the night more snow had fallen, obliterating all tracks. But he knew which way to go to pick up fresh ones. For three days, without putting in at any other house, he kept after the panthers. They separated. He got the one he followed.

For him a part of the stimulation afforded by hunting lay in enduring severe weather. One freezing morning Jim Yeldell, out hunting hogs horseback, came upon Ben Lilly wading waist-deep through swamp waters. "Jim," he called out, "I ran into a hog froze to death just now."

He never wore coat or overcoat in the winter, but did wear three or four wool shirts, which he changed by pulling off the one next to his undershirt and putting it over the one that had been outside. He held that the elements will cleanse any garment exposed to them.

One cold, damp fall night he crawled into a hollow cypress log, where he slept snug. The next morning he built a fire by the log. While he was eating his freshly parched corn, an immense rattlesnake, warmed by the fire, crawled out. Ben Lilly looked at him and said — so Boyd Williams heard him relate: "Brother, you didn't bother me last night. I went into your house, and you let me be. I won't bother you now, and I promise you I won't ever bother any of your folks."

The "promise" — if seriously made — was rash, and later experiences justified the promiser in taking it back. He was wary of the rattlesnake folks. After two days without food and in the rain in Arizona mountains in 1916, he started to enter a cave one night for shelter. "Found a Big Rattle snake," his diary says. "I Killed him and Told him he might have company. So I Took the rain in preference of a chance with a rattler."

There was in Arizona at this time another noted character who made a compact, which he seems to have kept, with rattlesnakes. "I was driving Jeff Milton from his ranch in the Huachuca Mountains to Tucson," Leslie H. Chamberlain wrote me from the Provost Marshal's Office at Oceanside, California, in 1946. "Seeing a rattlesnake in the road just ahead, I stopped the car and jumped out, drawing my six-shooter — but I did not shoot. Jeff Milton told me not to. He explained that while he was trailing down Bronco Bill Walters and his gang in Arizona mountains, he heard a strong buzzing in the rocks a good way above him. He knew that he had not disturbed the rattlesnake and he suspected that somebody else had. He ducked, skirted around, and discovered one of Bronco Bill's outlaws easing down the mountain to ambush him. He got his Winchester going in time to cut down Bronco Bill and to hold the two men with him. A rattlesnake had saved his life. After that he

[82]

regarded all rattlesnakes as his friends and would not kill one." *

Ben Lilly had several camping places in the Louisiana swamps, and his idea of a comfortable winter was to "lay out" with his dogs and Tutt Alford to cook for them, until spring softened the weather. Camp was more home to him than a house where dogs were unwelcome. Now and then grizzled Tom Bradley would join him. One winter he invited Henry Jackson and two other young fellows to come along.

"We struck camp where they had been camping for years," Henry Jackson recalled. "They had old bear skulls up in the forks of trees. That first evening we greeners got up wood and raked leaves to sleep on while Mr. Lilly and Bradley went out to investigate. They came in with news of plenty of sign. We all ate supper and then they commenced telling what a time they had had killing this one and that one, pointing towards the skulls. They made us believe there was a bear under every tree in the swamp. Mr. Lilly let me go with him on other hunts and I killed several. When men has bear-hunted together they have a different

* According to Evetts Haley, the rattlesnake saved Jeff Milton's life in another way. Anyhow, after this experience, Jeff the Just "would never kill a rattlesnake" or allow anybody else to kill one. "Let him go about his business," he would say. — J. Evetts Haley, *Jeff Milton: A Good Man with a Gun*, University of Oklahoma Press, Norman, 1948, 288–301, 385.

feeling for one another than just friends. I know I would have went any length for Mr. Lilly, and I believe he would for me."

But Ben Lilly was not what most men would agree on as a hunting companion. The average hunter hunts for pleasure. He does not find pleasure in trying to sleep in the cold without blankets, in filling his belly with husked corn — perhaps with only a killdeer shot at evening after a day of fasting or a disdained mudfish speared out of muddy water. He does not find sport or the healing powers of nature in staying wet all day and then, if he dries at night, drying under a cake of mud. His idea of life is not to reduce it to the starkness by which the most elemental animal exists. Ben Lilly was not a wild man of the woods. In many ways he was gentle and considerate of others. For him, however, hunting often meant leaving his own harsh camp farther behind than the average hunter leaves his comfortable home to "rough it" in a well-provisioned, prodigally fueled camp of dry tents, soft beds and moist bottles.

Aside from bears and panthers, alligators interested him most. Once at least, it is claimed, he managed to mount an alligator and to ride it in Jim Bowie style, gouging a thumb in each eye and with the other part of the hand pulling up on the mouth corners, thus securing his seat and in a manner bridling the brute. He tried catching alligators in bear traps, but the sliding movement of the animal generally throws a trap before a foot enters it. He harpooned alligators, roped a few, and snared more. He could imitate the whine of a puppy to entice alligators up for harpooning. One year he hunted alligators for hides to sell.

He was positively childish in his fondness for "fooling" with alligators. He built a dam across a slough running through his block of land at Mer Rouge and fenced in the pond; then he captured several big alligators and turned them loose in the enclosure. A hard freeze killed them all, their dens being too shallow for protection.

Near the Mark Harp home was a large cypress brake inhabited by numerous alligators. The biggest one — the biggest in Louisiana, it is said — was known as Old Lep. Ben Lilly was fond of him — after a fashion. When he visited the Harps, he nearly always got into a skiff and rowed out for a visit to Old Lep. Getting close to him, he would prod him with a pole, "just to see him roar." This alligator's mighty bellowing could be distinguished from that of all other alligators in the vicinity, and, hearing it, people would say, "Listen to Ben Lilly's Old Lep." A particular roar was regarded as a forecast of rain — and rain usually followed about two days after it was heard. One time Lilly caught Old Lep on shore and pitched a rope on him, drawing up the noose. The mighty bull, instead of playing on the line, went to rolling over and over up the rope. Lilly's hand became entangled in it and he was about, it seemed, to be drawn into the brute's mouth. He rammed his rifle barrel down it and shot, killing the source of his amusement.

Along in the '90's Ben Lilly drifted out of the cattle-trading business, as he had drifted out of farming, and became a timber man. Like other occupations, logging did not hold him away from hunting. It kept him deep in the woods, sometimes cutting down trees, hiring other men to cut, hauling the logs out in a heavy wagon drawn by sixteen oxen. He piled a yard full of logs against a railroad siding at Mer Rouge and another at Bonita. Each end of his logs was squared with a broadax and painted red. Most of the logs were black walnut. He did not know timber, however, and hauled in much that was at the time unmarketable. In the end he abandoned the two great stocks of black walnut. T. Y. Harp estimates that at present prices the timber thus abandoned would be worth at least $100,000. For years residents of Mer Rouge and Bonita cut the Ben Lilly black walnut into firewood and burned it.

Timber cutters are as rough as tradition has made them. "You ought to have your mouth washed out with soap and water," Ben Lilly would say to a foul-worded logger. "Get down, Jim, and hitch your cursing outside," he called in his soft voice to a loud man who rode up to his timber camp.

According to one story, Mary Lilly finally told her husband that if he ever left on another hunt, she hoped he would keep on going. One day towards the end of the year 1901, he transferred all of his property except five dollars to her, called his three children together, kissed them good-by, very affectionately kissed Mary good-by also, took his dogs and headed for the Tensas River, in Northeastern Louisiana.

In the dense, moist forests and canebrakes of the Tensas River basin were lairs from which no hunter of Ben Lilly's persistence, skill and endurance had yet harried the bears. He knew these lairs, for he had often been among them. Here to this day, despite draining and clearing, the rare ivory-billed woodpecker flashes his black and white wings in the tall trees and calls his startling cry. It is the bird that Ben Lilly seems to have felt nearest to. He kept a camp on the Tensas for a long time. On occasions he hunted for the market, especially ducks and geese. He would send wild turkeys, ducks, wild honey and other yieldings of the woods back home when opportunity came. He had a dog named Joe that was as expert as a bear at locating bee trees. For a brief while he went into the pig business, following in a wagon the wild razorbacks wherever acorns tolled them. The wagon was for hauling in the bacon. He made some money logging and sent it back home. He drifted across Red River and got among the Acadians of the great Atchafalaya swamps. The muskrats they trapped from pirogues never interested him. He was on Vermilion Bay. He never got too far away to write to his children. After he had been gone for nearly thirty years and was still sending back checks out of his earnings for killing predatory animals in New Mexico, he could say: "I can't remember ever speaking a cross word to my brothers or sisters, or to my father or mother. I am sure I never spoke a cross word to one of my children. They have never done anything that hurt my feelings."

Maybe sometimes he wanted to go back. If so, he wanted more to go on — always out, never in.

> White hands cling to the tightened rein,
>   Slipping the spur from the booted heel,
> Tenderest voices cry, "Turn again!"
>   Red lips tarnish the scabbarded steel,

High hopes faint on a warm hearth stone —
He travels the fastest who travels alone.

If not in these lines from Kipling, Ben Lilly would
have recognized himself in,

His neighbors' smoke shall vex his eyes, their voices
break his rest.

To the end of his remembering days Ben Lilly never
tired of recalling how he hunted with President
Theodore Roosevelt. He was hunting in Texas, headed
west, when a telegram summoned him and his dogs
to the elaborate presidential camp on Tensas Bayou,
where he arrived on Sunday, October 5, 1907.

Newspaper correspondents, lodged miles from
camp, had no direct contact with the President and
only limited contact with other members of his party,
but that did not prevent their sending out bulletins on
the progress of the royal hunt. A special correspondent
for the *Daily Picayune* of New Orleans held the front
page daily during the two weeks' siege of the bears.
On some days "Chief Huntsman" Ben Lilly — his sad,
ascetic, bearded face pictured by one remarkable
photograph — got publicity second to Teddy himself.
The approaching birth of an heir apparent to a nation's
throne has seldom been heralded with more certainty
of public interest than Roosevelt's approach to a bear.

On Sunday, of course, Lilly made no move remotely connected with hunting, but talk in camp of his "knowledge of every nook and cranny of the canebrakes" was a promise for the morrow. The morrow turned out to be fruitless, however. There were, as Ben Lilly well knew, too many dogs, scores of them, too many men, too much noise, too much ado all around. On a hunt like this, local bigwigs, political bigwigs especially, horn in.

On Tuesday it rained all day and everybody remained in camp except Ben Lilly. He "was out looking for sign and found it." There was talk of how "Lilly generally uses his knife in a close fight with a bear." He was not the only knife hunter present. Knife men from Mississippi as well as Louisiana had come with their packs. Like long-knifed Davy Crockett and other Southern bear hunters before them, it was a matter of principle with them not to stand by and see dogs killed in a fight with a bear but, when the mix-up got too close for shooting, to "wade in" with a knife. One of the company named Clark made a practice of calling his dogs off after they got a bear in close quarters and walking in against him alone. He told the President how he once tripped in some vines and was left hanging head down. The dogs answered his call for help and held the bear until he worked himself

[90]

loose. He knifed the bear, but after that he always carried a gun for emergencies.

There was talk of how General Wade Hampton of South Carolina used to prefer knifing to shooting, and stabbed "thirty or forty" bears. Roosevelt learned the details of a noted bear-and-man fight in which Dr. Monroe Hamberlin of Mississippi had arm and neck so crushed between the jaws of a monster he-bear that he died, though not before he had his dead antagonist weighed. It weighed 640 pounds. Crockett's prize bear weighed 617 pounds. Ben Lilly had no record of weights. He never encumbered himself with scales.

On Wednesday the Lilly dogs started a bear but the President was not at the right stand for a shot. A man from camp reported heavier firing than when Roosevelt's Rough Riders charged up San Juan Hill. Bears were said to be leaving the country. The President killed a buck, chased a wildcat, fished. Ben Lilly thought about as much of rabbits as he did of wildcats, regarded deer about as housewives regard butcher-shops, shot fish if he had to have one. He used to say, "Anybody can kill a deer. It takes a man to kill a varmint."

The week went by, and no bear for the President of the United States of America. Something seemed wrong with the management. On Saturday "Ben Lilly took charge of the hunt." Camp was changed. The fifty dogs in camp were a great disturbance to Lilly. He did not hunt on Sunday, but the reporters got a story as to how he trained his dogs, or, rather, how he once planned to train them: George Stivers was helping him drive cattle to Lake Providence. He had some young dogs along. After delivering the cattle, he and Stivers went to a big canebrake on Lost Island Plantation, where they killed a bear and skinned it. The skin gave Ben Lilly an idea.

Leaving Stivers to hold the dogs, he went into a neck of the dense cane, fitted the bearskin over his own body, and, on all fours, began threshing back towards Stivers and the dogs. It sounded to Stivers as if "the creation bear" were charging through the cane. He released the dogs and sicked them on. The beast kept coming. The dogs were having a hard time getting to it in the dense growth. They made up in noise what they lacked in skill, and the quarry's responding growls grew fiercer — so fierce that Stivers decided the thing wasn't Ben Lilly but a real bear. The dogs had certainly so decided.

In a low voice Stivers called out, "Ben, oh Ben, is that you?"

There was no answer and a cuffed dog howled.

[92]

Louder now, Stivers called, "Ben Lilly, is that you? Tell me."

Still there was no answer and the threshing around in the cane, accompanied by snarls, got nearer.

Raising his voice and his gun together, Stivers cried out, "By God, Ben Lilly, if that's you, you'd better say something, else I'm shore going to shoot."

This time there was an answer: "Don't shoot, George! Don't shoot! It's me, Ben Lilly." The earnest dogs had already bitten his ankles. He had to jerk the bearskin off to get rid of them. He decided this was not the best way to train bear dogs. . . .

At daylight on Tuesday, October 15, the thermometer stood at 40° and Teddy jumped into Bear Lake, swam a hundred yards out and back, rode his horse — and missed getting a bear. "Ben Lilly is such a wonder in the woods," the *Picayune* reported, "that the people here never tire of talking about him. While breakfast was being prepared the other morning, Lilly said he had lost his knife in the woods the night before several miles away. He took out in a trot and two hours later emerged from the thick canebrake with the knife. One of the hunting party said that if the McKinley Monument had been located in that brake it would have taken him a week to find it.

"The Lilly dogs have been in rather bad condition,

[93]

but Ben melted up a lot of lard and rubbed it on them. He said: 'A man must try to retain the respect of his dogs. If he gets so low-down a dog don't respect him, he's low sure enough.' "

On Thursday, October 17, dogs ran a big bear through cane into Bear Lake. It swam across and got away. Ben Lilly located fresh sign of another bear. Nothing is said about the matter, but the "Chief Huntsman" seems to have been relegated. Ben Lilly was a lone wolf, no manager of men, no executive. He was out of place in a big party of any kind. In not becoming a professional guide for big hunting parties, he considered his own limitations as well as a strong inclination — to be beholden to no man.

On Friday the President shot and killed a lean she-bear. Standing over the quarry, he yelled, danced, shook hands with men who came up. Ben Lilly was off locating fresh sign. Two hard-riding Mississippi planters got credit for the successful end of the chase.

On Sunday Roosevelt's hunt passed into history. A railroad siding was named for him. Camp broke at noon and all hunters set out for home "excepting Ben V. Lilly, who refused to break the Sabbath Day." He remained alone till Monday morning, when he headed back for his trapping grounds in Texas.

Somebody on the hunt — not Teddy, it seems — killed a cub bear. The Teddy bear fad was already popular; now it became the American craze. Representations of a bear cub became the chief American toy and doll as well as talisman for millions of adults. In the popular mind it has fixed Roosevelt the statesman next to Crockett as a man of bears. Crockett was an ignorant, though intelligent, backwoods bear-hunter; propaganda and the mobile eagerness of the American people for sensations had made him a public figure.

Ben Lilly never asked anybody to show him a bear. To find sign was with him the same, except for the time element, as finding the bear itself. No horseman, East or West, ever kept up with him in bear country. Roosevelt wore spurs. He was the last American of public consequence on horseback.

A man may think he can be all things, but he can't. The term "universal genius" is self-contradictory. The deepest man in history was but a lake, not an ocean. A man may prospect many fields; he puts his roots down deep only in one. Before Roosevelt got out of the Louisiana woods, the papers were headlining in boxcar letters one of the historic panics of Wall Street, and financiers were laying it to Roosevelt's "trust-busting" activities. Roosevelt hit the plat-

form with both heels, went to making speeches, receiv-
ing reporters, accommodating photographers. Despite
a lusty liking for the outdoors and despite millions of
Teddy bears that popularized his hunting articles and
books, he was more in his element chariot-racing
down Strenuous Life Avenue than in camping with
a man who belonged to the silent woods as essentially
as the bears themselves.

Roosevelt comprehended the surface of this man,
but the surface only. He summed him up as "a religious
fanatic." Fanatic he was, but a hunting — not a religious — fanatic. The demon that possessed him was of
the woods and mountains, not of theology. He had
no burning religious theory to deliver. He never made
the least attempt to impose his religious views on
others. His single mania for living with the wild beasts
in their jungles and for hunting them down was to
him as justifiable as that of the ancient Roman who
ended every speech, every thought, with three words
expressive of his never-varying reason for existing:
Delenda est Carthago. In defining as God's purpose his
own desire to hunt, the Chief Huntsman was not even
eccentric. Most men create God in their own image.
Boiled down, Ben Lilly's fanaticism and eccentricity as
respects religion consisted merely in the literal and
rigid fulfillment of the scriptural command to "keep

the Sabbath Day to sanctify it. . . . In it thou shalt
not do any work, thou, nor thy son, nor thy daughter,
nor thy manservant, nor thy maidservant, nor thine
ox, nor thine ass, nor any of thy cattle, nor the stranger
that is within thy gates; that thy manservant and thy
maidservant may rest as well as thou." If among millions of people who profess to keep the Sabbath Day
holy, a solitary man obeys the law to its last letter, he
may be odd, but oddness is not fanaticism. Lilly was
not one whit odder than Stonewall Jackson.*

While Charlie McEalrath was cow-driving for Ben
Lilly, he never heard of church. Billy Reneau, who

* "Jackson's religion entered into every action of his life. No
duty, however trivial, was begun without asking a blessing, or
ended without returning thanks. He had long cultivated, he said,
the habit of connecting the most trivial and customary acts of life
with a silent prayer. He took the Bible as his guide, and it is pos-
sible that his literal interpretation of its precepts caused many to
regard him as a fanatic. His observance of the Sabbath was hardly
in accordance with military usage. He never read a letter on that
day, nor posted one; he believed that the Government in carrying
the mails were violating a divine law, and he considered the sup-
pression of such traffic one of the most important duties of the
legislature. . . .

"'You appear much concerned,' he writes to his wife, 'at my
attacking on Sunday. I am greatly concerned too; but I felt it my
duty to do it, in consideration of the ruinous effects that might
result from postponing the battle until the morning. So far as I
can see, my course was a wise one; the very best that I could do
under the circumstances, though very distasteful to my feelings;
and I hope and pray that I may never again be circumstanced as on
that day. I believed that, so far as our troops were concerned,
necessity and mercy both called for the battle.'" – Colonel G. F.
R. Henderson, *Stonewall Jackson and the Civil War*, London, 1913,
I, 61–62, 257.

worked for him at another time, claims that he had or-
ders to go to church on Sunday. At one time, they
say, Ben Lilly would walk to church if it was not more
than five miles away, but he would not have a horse
break its rest to convey him. Yes, "Ben was a notionous sort of feller." Without violating the Sabbath, he
could on that day add to his reputation of being "a
character" as well as on any other day. Averaged up
and down, he had no concern for churches or prelates.
He did not belong to any church. His church, like his
home, was where he was — in the woods. He admired
the noted revival preacher — and showman — Sam
Jones. He could quote from at least one of the syndi-
cated sermons of Thomas De Witt Talmage. After he
was past fifty he read the Bible considerably.

Out of sight of other men, he was a rigid discipli-
narian of himself. He did not pray in public, did not
aloud express thanks for bread. Nor did he go around
thanking God that "I am not as other men are." Spir-
itual resources within himself gave him satisfaction —
along with the reputation of being original.

In an illustrated article on the hunt, Roosevelt described this odd man as "spare, full-bearded, with mild,
gentle, blue eyes and a frame of steel and whipcord.
I never met any other man so indifferent to fatigue
and hardship. He equaled Cooper's Deerslayer in

woodcraft, in hardihood, in simplicity – and also in loquacity. The morning he joined us in camp, he had come on foot through the thick woods, followed by his two dogs,* and had neither eaten nor drunk for twenty-four hours; for he did not like to drink the swamp water. It had rained hard throughout the night and he had no shelter, no rubber coat, nothing but the clothes he was wearing, and the ground was too wet for him to lie on; so he perched in a crooked tree in the beating rain, much as if he had been a wild turkey. But he was not in the least tired when he struck camp; and, though he slept an hour after breakfast, it was chiefly because he had nothing else to do, inasmuch as it was Sunday, on which day he never hunted or labored. He could run through the woods like a buck, was far more enduring, and quite as indifferent to weather, though he was over fifty years old. He had trapped and hunted throughout almost all the half century of his life, and on trail of game he was as sure as

* Writing to his daughter Ethel from camp on Tensas Bayou, Oct. 6, 1907 (*Theodore Roosevelt's Letters to His Children,* edited by John Bucklin Bishop, New York, 1927, pages 209–210), Roosevelt calls Lilly "a religious fanatic" who "quotes the preacher Talmage continually" and says that Lilly arrived "with one dog." S. L. Carrico, now of San Antonio, from whose camp on the Texas coast Lilly set out for the hunt in Louisiana, says that he left "with his pack of four hounds." The number does not matter. The conflicting reports merely show how a biographer must put down what he thinks is right despite "the evidence." Incidentally, Roosevelt spells Lilly's name two of the wrong ways.

CHAPTER V

In Texas and Mexico

IN 1904, Ned Hollister of the Biological Survey reported to Washington headquarters from Louisiana: "Mr. B. V. Lilly, who accompanied us on our hunt in Madison and Carroll parishes, is said by everyone to be the best hunter in Mississippi and Louisiana. He is truthful to an extreme."

Hollister was a first-rate scientist, as his studies on birds, muskrats, prairie dogs and other animal life attest. Ben Lilly admired him, and the association marked a turning point in his life. It was not until years later that he drew a salary from the Biological Survey, but he was now engaged to send in specimens. He learned to prepare skins and skeletons correctly. In the National Museum at Washington he is represented today by various specimens, among them otter, ivory-billed woodpecker, wolf, deer and bear — from Louisiana, Texas, Mexico, Arizona, New Mexico.

Biologists whom he came to know extended his views towards wildlife, though they did not convert him into a conservationist. His interest in bears never "grew to overshadow interest in the game," as did that of William H. Wright, who, after having studied the grizzly to hunt him, hunted to study him and then wrote the most informative book yet printed on that animal. Yet it is doubtful if any field naturalist has ever learned as much about bears and panthers as Ben Lilly learned during more than a half-century's hunting.

In time his observations entered the records of various naturalists. Concerning the passenger pigeon, Harry C. Oberholser's *The Bird Life of Louisiana* (1938) notes: "Apparently the latest report of the species in the State is by the well-known hunters, B. V. Lilly and I. H. Alford [Tutt, the Negro so often with Lilly] of Prairie Mer Rouge, who informed Ned Hollister in 1904 that up to the preceding winter they had seen a few wild pigeons annually. During the winter of 1902–1903 he saw about 40 or 50 birds." Concerning the ivory-billed woodpecker, the same work notes: "B. V. Lilly collected two specimens for the United States National Museum, on March 10, 1906, on Cow Bayou in Iberville Parish." In Vernon Bailey's *Mammals of New Mexico* (1931), a specimen of Nelson's grizzly and the type specimen of the Apache grizzly are credited to B. V. Lilly. In Florence Merriam Bailey's *Birds of New Mexico* (1928), Lilly is cited on

wild turkeys. His tracks are to be found in C. Hart
Merriam's *Review of the Grizzly and Big Brown Bears
of North America* (1918). Prentiss N. Gray's *Records
of North American Big Game* (1932) on one page
alone gives the measurements of six specimens of black
bear sent by Lilly to the National Museum.

Although by no means an authority on birds, he had
fair knowledge of the water fowl of Louisiana; his
information on grasses, flowers and shrubs was beyond that of most men of the woods and ranges. However, his never-ebbing passion to know all facts, direct
and indirect, relating to bears and panthers made other
creatures accessory. His interest in the ubiquitous
piñon jay of the Western mountains was largely confined to what this inquisitive bird might tell him of
movements in the woods beyond his view. *Amigo de
los venados* (friend of the deer), Mexican hunters call
the bird, because it always says something when it de-
tects movement. It says something about a moving deer,
a bear clawing into a rotten log for grubs, a panther
sneaking towards a buck, as well as about a moving
man. To Ben Lilly, the always charming tassel-eared
squirrel was primarily another sentinel.

Early in 1906, with no more in his purse than an
apostle was supposed to have, with no scrip at all,
without even a dog, and, seemingly, with a mind made

up never to return home, Ben Lilly, soon to be fifty years old, entered the Big Thicket of Texas against the Louisiana line. Thenceforth he was to be as detached geographically as he had always been inwardly from the tie-ropes of family and home opinion. There is no evidence that he ever wanted or ever had a fling with wine, women or song. He wanted to live stark free of all human restraints — and to hunt. He wore his beard, drank water, lived on squirrel meat and corn bread, and went his wonted way.

The original Big Thicket of Texas lay for a hundred miles up and down the Sabine River with an average width of perhaps fifty miles. By the time Ben Lilly entered it, agriculture and lumbering had eaten deeply into it, but it was still big. Since his time, oil and the ruthless paper mill industry have blackened and mutilated more of it, but it is still the Big Thicket of luxuriant plant life.

Some of the few settlers living in log cabins on the natural clearings wanted to forget and some wanted to be forgotten. They supplemented the supply of fish, game meat and wild fruits in season with patches of corn and sweet potatoes. Some led bestial lives; not one was so naturally primitive as the serene hunter out in the forest apart from them. He had seen and was to see many rough men; their roughness and coarseness no more entered his nature than the lusts of the legions she led entered into Joan of Arc. "My father," says Arden Hooks of Kountze, Texas, "was passing fond of rough tales. He said that Mr. Lilly was always good-naturedly embarrassed by them. In my youthful eyes, he seemed to be a man who knew many of the answers but reserved them to himself. His open face radiated cheerfulness and high spirits held in check."

He hunted considerably with Ben Hooks, who gave him a cur and a Scottish terrier; he taught Hooks how to temper hunting knives to the proper drake-neck color. He was hunting especially for a specimen bear for the Biological Survey. He said he would not mind waiting a year to get it. He got it along in December; it was his one hundred and eighteenth, somebody remembers his saying. One of his fellow hunters was Judge Louis B. Hightower, who said that Lilly was the only man he had ever met who talked all the time and never stretched the truth. Judge Hightower was another original character. He used to keep from twenty-five to fifty hounds, feeding them on wild beef and hot-water corn bread. Although judge of the District Court in his part of Texas, he never moved to town. Offered an appointment as federal judge, he refused, saying, "I want to die with my friends and my dogs and live where I can step off my own front gallery and take a leak without anybody's looking."

When Lilly headed out of the Big Thicket on Christmas Day, 1906, he said there were only fifteen bears left in it and not more than forty in all Louisiana and Mississippi. He traveled southwest until he came to the Big Caney bottoms on the Texas coast, between the Brazos and Colorado rivers. Construction of the St. Louis and Brownsville Railway across the region had just been completed, but the alligators, bears and deer of the woods and millions of wintering ducks and geese of the swamps and open marshes had hardly been disturbed by human hordes later to follow oil field, factory and other development along the Gulf shores. East of Baytown, S. L. Carrico of San Antonio and his brother were clearing a five-thousand-acre ranch to be sold in small surveys to home-seekers. One day a Negro laborer told them that a strange trapper was camped near Old Ocean, a noted tract of about 10,000 acres of primeval land.

In an account written for me, Mr. Carrico says:

"I found Mr. Lilly's camp, introduced myself, and invited him to camp with us. He seemed to enjoy talking and during the next year or so he paid us frequent visits but would never stay long. He could not rest in a bed, he said. He had no horse or other means of conveyance except shanks' mare. He wore high shoes, and when he got a new pair would cut holes in their

sides, 'to let the water out.' He always spoke in a
gentle voice and, although he was as powerful as an
ox, his movements were gentle. I never heard him use
other than polite language. He had a clean mind. He
was more than courteous in the Old South manner;
he had a natural dignity and was always considerate of
the rights and feelings of others. However free in talking, he reserved his private affairs and his soul.

"A Negro helping him around his camp reported
that one morning after Mr. Lilly started to skin a
bobcat, he stopped, wiped his knife, sheathed it,
grabbed his gun, called his dogs, and, not saying a
word, put out through the woods at a dog-trot. Three
days later, without a word of explanation, he walked
back into camp toting a bearskin. Mr. Lilly later told
us that skinning a bobcat made him suddenly remember a bear trap he had set down near Matagorda Bay,
and he thought he had better go look at it.

"One time some Boone Settlement Negroes were
trying to load a 400-pound bear they had killed into a
wagon when Mr. Lilly came along. They had tied one
end of a rope around the bear's haunches, thrown the
other end over a limb, and were heaving away without being able to lift the carcass off the ground. Mr.
Lilly simply set all the Negroes to pulling in the slack
while he alone lifted. With one powerful lift he raised

the bear clear of the ground. They took in the slack, he gave another lift, and soon the bear was dangling above the wagon bed. The Negroes never stopped talking about this feat of strength.

"One time Mr. Lilly came to our camp, on his way to Bay City, carrying a pack of skins weighing fully 125 pounds. He would not sit down, would not even put his pack down. It was summertime. Behind the mess shack we had cantaloupes and watermelons covered with wet Spanish moss to keep them cool, also a tub full of ripe tomatoes. Mr. Lilly tarried about an hour, standing up, pack-laden, and while he talked he ate a dozen or so big tomatoes, two or three cantaloupes, and a whole watermelon.

"We boys, eager to hear of any recent hunting exploits, questioned him as to when he had got his last bear. For a little while he seemed to be trying to recollect, and then said, 'Oh, I got one this morning.' It took us a long time to dig the facts out of him.

"He had set a heavy steel trap in a cornfield down near Boone Settlement. A bear had walked into it and then ripped out the stake to which the trap chain was fastened and made off a short distance into a dense thicket of rattan and wild peach. When Mr. Lilly got to the site, he found a group of Negroes raising bedlam and wondering what to do to get the bear. The

Lilly hounds were so well trained that they did nothing without his command. He left them on the outside of the thicket, took his gun, and crawled in on hands and knees until he got within twenty feet of the bear. He then worked his body against the rattan vines on both sides to clear out enough space for free movement. When he had the vines worked back and down, he moved over as far to the right as he could get and purposely antagonized the bear with a shot that merely wounded him. The bear charged and when it was nearly on him, Mr. Lilly jumped to the left as far as the thicket would permit. As the bear rushed past, he grabbed him around the neck, jumped on his back, pulled his big knife, and stabbed him. Bear and man went down together. By the time the Negroes got to him, he had pulled himself free. Meanwhile his dogs had bayed mournfully but stayed behind him about fifty feet, precisely where he had told them to stay.

"One morning about three o'clock I set out with Mr. Lilly to cut a bee tree twenty miles south of camp. We were equipped with two buckets, about fifty feet of rope, a six-and-a-half-foot crosscut saw, and two guns. Just as we started sawing on the bee tree, a dead live oak, it began to rain. We sawed steadily on that tree, the water that ran down the trunk acting as a lubri-

cant to our saw, until about four o'clock in the afternoon. Then the tree crashed to the ground.

"Contrary to specific instructions, I slapped at the
first bee that landed on my face and then started running up a muddy trail through about eighteen inches
of water. The whole hive took out after me, and I was
stung twelve or fifteen times before I threw myself
face down in the muddy water and stayed there as
long as I could hold my breath. Mr. Lilly finally
coaxed me back, laughing like a crazy man all the
while, and induced me to come to where he was calmly
eating big gobs of honey and blowing the bees away
from his mouth and off his nose."

From the Old Ocean country — and this was to be
the last lowland he would ever hunt in — Ben Lilly
went west to the Texas border. He crossed the Rio
Grande at Eagle Pass, in July, 1908, and did not stop
until he was in the Santa Rosa Mountains of northern
Coahuila. Bears were thick in the "Santy Roses," as
he called them, and for a few months he killed venison
for a mining camp. He sold jerked venison to a Mexican store in Múzquiz, from which he also shipped
hides. Here Ernest F. Black, manager of the Mariposa
Ranch, met him and invited him to come to his range
and hunt.

They rode out to the Mariposa together, and when they got to the gate from which headquarters could be seen, about two miles away, Ben Lilly exclaimed, "You didn't tell me you had your womenfolks there."

"How do you know they are there?" Black asked.

"It takes womenfolks to grow flowers and vines."

He established camp at a spring, but occasionally ate at the house, and the "womenfolks" thought he smelled mighty "strong." He prepared hides and skulls to ship to the Smithsonian Institution at Washington. He killed so many deer that Manager Black saw he would not have any left if the hunter remained much longer. He prepared to move on, northwest. He had acquired an old pack mare on which were packed his traps, corn meal and a bucket of wild honey. She took fright at a concrete water tank at Mariposa headquarters, stampeded and mixed honey, meal and traps all together on the ground.

To this day the high, rough and vast Sierra del Burro country, across the Rio Grande from the Big Bend National Park of Texas, is one of the most remote and thinly populated areas of the continent. Cerro Del Carmen and adjacent mountains in the range are clad with pines; against them jut bleak foothills; out from the foothills sprawl wastes of alkali deserts supporting nothing bigger than greasewood.

This desert land makes that horror of thirst and summer heat called the Bolsón de Mapimí. In Ben Lilly's time the Fronteriza Mine, in mountains about thirty miles from the Rio Grande, worked hundreds of peon Mexicans. Competing with the cheapest kind of labor, Lilly supplied them with antelope and deer meat. He hired burro drivers to pack goatskins of bear grease into the village of Boquillas on the Rio Grande. He could speak hardly a word of the country's language.

In the region was another remarkable man of the *campo*, who had, however, the perspective that comes from reading the classics. He had a small ranch and knew the lore about cattle, horses, rattlesnakes, deer, eagles, javelinas, jaguars and *vaquero* (Mexican cowboy) life much better than he knew the business of ranching. His real interest was collecting documents and writing a history of the Mexican frontier. A part of this history is a bulky manuscript entitled *Around the Camp Fire*, which he allowed me to copy. A few pages in it deal with Ben Lilly. In quoting from them I salute the memory of their author — Don Alberto Guajardo.

"El Señor Lilly spent his Sundays lying in the shade of a tree and reading the Bible. He was more interested in finding new species of animals than in just killing anything he saw. He often forgot his only camping utensils, a tin pan and an old tin cup, and left them at some water hole. When he found honey in a rock crevice or a hollow tree, he would gouge out handfuls of it and eat it from his hand, right there.

"One very cold evening he killed a large female bear and skinned it. He spread a cured deerskin under a rocky ledge, lay down on it and covered with the fresh bearskin. Like all hunters who sleep out in the wilds, he had his rifle, loaded and the trigger on the safety catch, beside him. He told me that he was sleeping very warm and sound when he felt something nuzzling the bearskin over him and heard a growl. Quickly he drew away, jabbed the muzzle into the intruder's breast and fired until he had emptied the magazine of his rifle. It was dark, but he felt the target with his muzzle when he started shooting. He showed me the perforated skin of the bear he killed. It was a male — mate to the female he had killed not long before he lay down to sleep."

Ben Lilly spent perhaps a year in this region. He worked on west into the state of Chihuahua and got down almost as far as Chihuahua City. He killed wild turkeys that he considered the largest in North America. "It is all such an enormous country," he wrote, "that a man has to be an expert to hunt successfully.

[113]

Game may be plentiful in a certain locality one season and scarce the next. The hunter must do like the wild animals — travel and see where the food and water will be good. Year-olds do not incline to migrate like older animals."

On a mule trail — the *camino real*, "royal road," hundreds of years old — that corkscrews across western Chihuahua and down to the Yaqui River in Sonora, I once spread my bedroll at a location called La Quiparita. Here a fine spring of water flows out into a creek with low banks; "parks" between pine woods afford grass, and there is rich and strong grass on a mesa not far away. While we boiled daylight coffee we heard wild turkeys gobbling, and a little later saw a buck cross a glade. One may ride all day in that country and not meet another man on mule or burro and not see the smoke from a single human habitation. A north-and-south trail crosses the Chihuahua-Sonora trail at La Quiparita. It is a very noted camp ground and the finest I have ever camped at. I don't know whether Ben Lilly ever passed that way or not. I passed seventeen years after he had left Mexico. There was a legend among the few Pima Indians and Mexicans of the region that a grizzly bear with a white star in his breast claimed La Quiparita as his own, attacking all travelers who stopped there and surviving all attempts to kill him — until a bearded *Americano* came along.

This was, and is, one of the many bears of Mexican folklore — a half-brother perhaps to Juan Oso, the half-bear and half-man hero. He sounds like the bear that A. L. Inman remembers Mr. Lilly's telling about. Most human beings may be divided into two classes: those who forget and those who have constructive memories. Inman is the kind of man who does not forget.

According to his memory, a grizzly of the Sierra Madre had formed the habit of killing and eating children. Mexicans bold enough to hunt it never met anything but bad luck. Some families moved out of the bear's range. Then Ben Lilly came along. When authorities saw that he had no fear, they offered him a thousand pesos to kill the grizzly — just as their ancestors had once paid gringos bounties on the scalps of Apaches.

Several days after he set a heavy trap, he found it gone. The tracks of the grizzly that had stepped into it were fresh, and as he followed them he expected to see him rise at any moment. He moved on the trail slowly, stealthily; but he moved. When he got his first view of the bear, the mighty animal was standing upright, across a gulch, watching intently. The bear's eyes had caught the motion of his pursuer maybe a second before the pursuer saw him. An instant later Lilly saw the monster gather trap and clog into a fore-arm and crash into the growth towards him. As he emerged, Lilly began shooting his .33 rifle, putting, he felt sure, a bullet into him at every shot. Still the grizzly came on. The last shot in the rifle magazine had been fired, Lilly had pulled his long knife, and then, only ten feet away, the bear dropped dead.

This bear story is not found in any of Ben Lilly's writings. I give it as an item in the Ben Lilly legend. No man is to be held responsible for everything that other people quote him as having said. Ben Lilly's habitual truthfulness is expressed in a saying that he often repeated: "Before you make definite statements about wild animals get supporting facts." If asked whether a panther "screams like a terrified woman," he would reply: "Maybe so. I have heard one squall and spit like a tomcat. I have never heard anything like a woman's scream from a panther." In 1943, his old chief, Dr. A. K. Fisher of the Biological Survey, wrote that in talking to scientific men and in official reports Lilly had always been factual concerning the behavior of animals, though "when he was with a crowd telling stories, he often shot with a long bow. . . . It worries me a little now to meet statements attributed to him by others that differ from those made to me. I checked up on him and never found any sign of falsehood in him." *

The Madero Revolution, which was to overthrow the people-strangling Diaz government, began a year before Lilly left Mexico. Its only effect on him was to shorten his supply of ammunition. An anecdote of this period came to me by letter from a man in Arizona:

"Lauro S. Kempher, half Spanish and half Irish, had been at the University of Madrid, then Oxford, and finally Annapolis. After acting as agent for a British lumber company in Chihuahua, he went to making cannon out of box-car axles for the Maderos. One evening just as he was about to pitch camp he came upon a bearded man seated with his back to a tree bradding deer-skin soles on his worn shoes. After passing the time of day with him, Kempher noticed that he was using brads at least half an inch long. 'Say,' he said, 'aren't those nails going all the way through?' Ben Lilly replied, 'I calculate they are. They kind of keep my feet from slipping around.' "

There may be a few exceptions to Robert Louis Stevenson's saying that every man wants to be regarded as a rake. Perhaps even fewer men do not at some time wish to be "a character." "I like original

* Letters from A. K. Fisher, Washington, D. C., to Monroe Goode, Dallas, Texas, May 14, 1943, and June 1, 1943.

characters," Balzac said. "I am one." Though men were scarce where Ben Lilly chose to range, the percentage of odd fishes among them was high. When he and one of the other oddities met, they delighted in each other. It was only courteous for each side to make some demonstration for the benefit of the other. One American in Mexico saw Ben Lilly lather himself with soap after a bath and then dress. He explained that sweat mixing with the lather would keep him clean.

He worked west until he was close to the Sonora line; he came out of Mexico into the southwest corner of New Mexico. This was early in 1911.* He was soon south of the border again, following one of the notabilities of his career. His own relation follows.†

"I started out about nine o'clock in the morning

* In an article published in the *Producer*, July, 1928, Lilly gives the date of his emergence from Mexico as 1910. He had forgotten. He entered Mexico in 1908, and he later made several statements to the effect that he remained in that country about three years. Vernon Bailey's *Mammals of New Mexico* (Washington, D. C., 1931, page 361) establishes the date: "On March 10, 1911, Lilly started this bear in the Animas Mountains in extreme southwestern New Mexico and followed it south through the San Luis Mountains into Chihuahua, across into Sonora, and back into Chihuahua before it was finally killed. Lilly was sure that he was following the same bear all the time, because it had lost two toes from one foot and made a track easily recognized."

† Published in the *Producer*. See sources given at end of this book. Mr. Lilly's writing was, I am sure, revised by an editor for printing. In the interest of clarity, and with the benefit of Stokley Ligon's recollections of Lilly's oral accounts, together with facts given by Vernon Bailey, I have made further revisions.

from my camp on the Diamond A Ranch in the Animas Mountains of New Mexico. Before long I found the tracks of two lions — a full-grown female and a half-grown animal. The tracks seemed to be about a week old. I had no hounds, only an Airedale dog. I also found the track of a full-grown brown grizzly. I could tell that he was brown, because I found brown hair on a bush that he had rubbed on. His tracks showed plainly that two toes were missing on a front foot. I worked on the track until dark. That night I went to my camp. Next morning I was out at daylight. I soon tracked the bear up. He had been eating sotol. When bears come out of hibernation, they are especially fond of sotol and the yucca called 'bear grass.' This fellow had eaten off two or three sotol heads, and had gone into brush so dense that it was impossible to see a bear even at a distance of twenty steps. I soon found the bed where he had lain that night; but he was gone. The Airedale asked to be excused when he smelled the bear's bed. He stayed away behind me.

"I tracked that bear until dark, when I built a fire and lay down to sleep. That night, as I saw next morning, the bear waded down a branch of the river for a long distance. I found where he had come out and had made a bed and lain down in it. Then he struck out for another day's travel. He went to a big hole that

[119]

on another trip he had scratched in the ground and covered with brush he bit down around it. After making this nest he seemed to have stayed in it over a week. Now he knew that I was tracking him and he kept going. I came to the carcass of a two-year-old steer. The way the small bushes were torn up showed he had tussled with the steer and wallowed him more than usual for a grizzly, which generally kills a cow brute right on the spot. He did not eat one mouthful of the steer, but struck out for Mexico. I followed him until he crossed the line; then I came back and waited a couple of weeks.

"While waiting, I went out to buy two burros, carrying an empty shotgun to trade for them. The man I went to see did not want to sell. On the way to camp, I looked for lion tracks. I had a young, unbroken hound with me. He seemed fond of running rabbits; so I let him chase rabbits. Soon I noticed him running hard down a hill and making a growling noise. I ran over a rise of ground for a clear view and saw that a full-grown female lion was after him. She had stopped and was humped up. I tried to run up on her and hit her with the empty gun. She broke away, with me and the dog after her. She ran up a tree, jumped out, and ran up another tree. I chunked her out with rocks. She treed again. I chunked her out.

"The rock I threw at her in the sixth tree she took to struck her in the mouth and stunned her slightly. The tree was low. I sprang up in it, grabbed her by the tail and jerked. We hit the ground all in a bundle together. The lion struck out, running downgrade, with me gaining on her. I had picked up a longish green pine stick, and with it I struck her on the back as she was passing over a small log. She sprang at me. I broke the pine stick in two over her head. She kept coming. I broke the stick five times over her head. Then I grabbed up a rock that would weigh about six pounds and pounded her on the side of her head. She fell at my feet, apparently dead. My pocketknife had a blade two and a quarter inches long, and I tried to stick this into her heart.

"I sat down, and the dog came up. He had been afraid to come up while I was chunking the lion, and he did not come near at any time while I was fighting. Now I made him bite her. I thought it would do the dog some good. He took two or three bites on her hind legs. Up she came and made for me. I grabbed up a big rock and gave a blow on the side of her head as she grabbed at me. That downed her. I pounded her on the head until the skull was crushed. I then reached her heart with the little knife. She measured six feet, eight inches long.

"In two or three days I went down to the United States soldiers' camp on the border. I told the officer in charge that I wanted to go over on the Mexican side to hunt a brown grizzly I had trailed to the line several days before. He said he would send two men with me. Not long after we struck out, I found the bear's tracks. About two o'clock that afternoon one soldier said to me, 'We've got all the bear hunting we want. Let's go to camp.' I said, 'You all go. I will find a good place to trap that bear before I leave these mountains.' Then they said good-by. Three days later I went to their camp and told them I had two bears hanging up in the mountains. The captain sent men and horses with me to bring in the meat.

"The brown grizzly with two toes off his front foot was still missing. I went back after him, killed a female lion on the route, and found that he had taken my trap. He traveled a rough country, dragging the trap over rocks. He wore the chain and clog off the trap. I followed him for several days, into Sonora and back into Chihuahua. He was making for his New Mexico range when I killed him late on a Saturday evening. I had chased him in three states and two countries. His front tusks were worn to the gums, both above and below. That was why he had trouble killing cattle. He was the oldest bear I ever killed. The

Biological Survey people called him a Nelson grizzly.

"On this same hunt, I killed the largest and also the oldest black female bear I have ever seen. The four large tusks called the holders were worn off, the same as on the brown male. The front teeth in both the upper and the lower jaws were worn down to the bone. I sent her hide and skull to the National Museum along with the grizzly's."

CHAPTER VI

Master Sign-reader of the Rockies

AT Animas, New Mexico, a mere trading post not
far north of the Mexican boundary, between the
Continental Divide and the Arizona line, Ben Lilly
found George Stivers running a store. He told his old
friend that he had about quit playing practical jokes.
In crossing the Continental Divide of America, Lilly
had crossed the Continental Divide of his own life. The
Western slopes were to be far more satisfactory to him
than the Eastern swamps had been. At the age of fifty-
five he was entering upon a career that added respect to notability and that ripened his knowledge of
animals and deepened his contentment in solitudes.

That career was killing predatory animals out of an
enormous territory of mountains, canyons and forests that instead of closing in opens out. The bears and
panthers that he had since boyhood pursued out of
a passion for hunting and killing now assumed the
proportions of primary enemies to mankind's thriving.
A single grizzly of the Rockies loomed above whole

[124]

herds of black bears in the swampy East. Wolves were an aside to Ben Lilly always. He arrived in New Mexico at a time when ranchers were becoming especially active against the destroyers of their stock, and in that activity were about to receive, beginning in 1914, powerful aid from the federal government. Henceforth he would be paid well for what during most of his life he had done at a loss. A career that had been something of a ne'er-do-well's folly now graduated into professional dignity. With renewed assurance of his mission in life, the lover of the wild went on annihilating it.

His first hunting for bounty was on the big Diamond A Ranch in the Animas Mountains. His pack of dogs was soon built up. He "found and killed 13 lions, some nice grizzlies and 12 bear," and a few lobo wolves. He was hoping for a jaguar. In 1912, with five hounds and five burros, he moved north to Clifton, in eastern Arizona, and adjacent territory. In one week he killed six bears and four lions and had the idea of making good money by collecting ten dollars a head from the county. He found, however, that in order to collect public money he must produce not only the animal's scalp but a witness to the killing. No cowboy would follow him around on foot as witness.

As he hunted, he kept count of the carcasses of dead

cattle and horses, many of them in rough places pene-
trated by "pioneer cattle" but never seen by men on
horseback. The bones of a grown animal, he observed,
last longer than those of a young one. He inclined to
attribute all carcasses to attacks by predators, overlooking the inevitability of stock losses from disease,
accident, undernourishment, and other causes for
which predators are not responsible. He told ranchers
that they were losing 20 per cent of their stock to
bears and lions and that paying him bounties was
economy. According to his figures — hardly too low
— each bear and lion prowling the range killed on the
average five hundred dollars' worth of stock a year. A
few stockmen who learned that no witness could be
more relied upon than Ben Lilly's own quiet word or-
ganized to pay him bounties for whatever stock-killers
he reported having exterminated.

The United States Forest Service was doing a limited amount of predatory control work, and Ben Lilly
got a job in the Apache National Forest as guard-
trapper at seventy-five dollars a month. But working
under any kind of boss was not his idea of the pur-
suit of liberty. Although there was, and is, a law pro-
tecting bears as game animals, to him all bears were
guilty. A bear may start out eating beef from the
kill of another bear or of a lion, he said, but after that

first taste he becomes like a man who has once eaten oysters: after the first bait, he hunts for the choice food. Why wait till a bear has killed before killing him? Here again, his philosophy was in accordance with his desires, also with his interest in collecting bounties. It was contrary to the Biological Survey's policy of killing only those bears proved to be guilty of killing stock.

For six or eight years he hunted back and forth across the Arizona-New Mexico line, up and down the San Francisco and Blue rivers, extending his range eastward and northward as he cleaned out the lions and bears. During these years he averaged perhaps fifty lions and bears a year, collecting sometimes as much as fifty dollars a scalp, often less. He found the Mormon ranchers hard to collect from. Some ranchers, anxious to clear their ranges, supplemented organization bounties with private bonuses.

In 1916 he began working sporadically for the United States Biological Survey. The Survey paid him one hundred dollars a month, a salary above that paid to regular trappers. He worked off and on for the Survey for four years, but always preferred to be his own boss. He thought he could make more money independently, and he had become proud of his financial success. He did not approve of the Survey's strict prohibition against killing deer out of season. A game warden who arrested him for violating it found all the ranchers agreeing with Ben Lilly that any lion he killed would destroy more deer in one year than hunter and dogs would eat while tracking down several lions.

Of the Survey men — and all whom he knew in the field were his friends — he probably felt closest to J. Stokley Ligon, who was for a time his supervisor. He had doubts about some of the office men in Washington. Once, a story goes, after reporting to headquarters that he had spent this day and that day and another day "cold-trailing," he received word from Washington to "quit cold-trailing and hunt hot trails." Ed Steele saw the cold-trailer just after he had received the letter and heard him say, "I guess I know as much about hunting lion as they do in Washington." He resigned right there.

On April 3, 1913, in the White Mountains of Arizona, he made what he considered the narrowest escape of his life. The narrative is in his own words.

"I struck this grizzly on Blue River and followed him for three days in snow. In places the snow had frozen and glazed over so that the bear did not make a visible track. In other places it was soft and waist deep. During the three days I did not have one mouthful to eat. I was wearing over my underclothes only a pair of blue cotton pants, a blue shirt and a light cotton sweater. I kept from freezing at night by building fires and sitting up by them.

"Three times at very long ranges I shot this bear in the same hip while he was running from me. I had a slow-track dog tied to my waist. Once we came to a cave the bear had denned in the winter preceding. It was about eight feet wide and about sixteen feet back. At the mouth were six layers of black dirt between layers of snow, showing that the bear had dragged out earth that many times during the season of snowfall. This is just one instance of evidence that hibernating bears come out for short whiles during the winter. They will drink water while out but will not take a mouthful of food. Another grizzly I trailed in the Escalder [Escudilla] Mountains in Arizona had made twelve trips in and out of his cave during his lay-up.

"The wounded grizzly had left lots of fresh blood at his old den, but I knew it was not from any vital part. About three hundred yards east of the den I saw blood again, where the grizzly had scratched snow out of one of his summer beds and laid down. The trail worked on into thick spruce undergrowth. I looked to one side, getting ready to fire. Then right in front of my body, fifteen feet away, the bear popped out, charging me. My first shot hit him center in the breast; that checked him. My second shot was under the eye, about three feet away. He fell against my side. I was bogged in snow waist-deep. I couldn't see the bear's head. He seemed to be drawing deep breaths. I fired another shot for his heart. I was wearing a knife eighteen inches long. I drove it for the heart. That finished him. It had been a test of endurance as well as a narrow escape.

"I took careful measurements of this bear, according to government standards. He measured nine foot from the tip of his nose to the end of his tail; eight foot around the body. He stood five foot, eight inches high. His hind foot was twelve inches long and seven inches wide across the pad. On the top side, his claws were five inches long and at the base each of them was as wide as a man's finger. His ankles, both front and rear, measured fourteen inches around. His skull was eighteen inches long. There wasn't any way of weighing him. He was the largest bear and made the largest track of any I know of having been killed in the Rocky Mountains. I sent the skull and the hide to Washington.

"After this bear died, I felt weak. My dogs and I both needed water. There was some under ice not far away, and we started to it. On the way we struck a lion track very fresh. I felt like a new man and took out in a run. The lion was soon treed and killed. We got water and went back to the grizzly bear. After I skinned him, the dogs and I had a good meal. I wrapped up in the skin by the carcass and slept as warm as if I were in a stove.

"I have read J. C. Adams's experiences with grizzlies [*The Adventures of James Capen Adams, Mountaineer and Grizzly Bear Hunter of California*, by Theodore H. Hittell]. When the subject of grizzlies' fighting comes up, I like to be able to call attention to what another man has seen. I have read Wright's book on grizzlies [*The Grizzly Bear*, by William H. Wright]. He liked to leave the impression that grizzlies are not fighters. I find a wounded grizzly of mature age more than willing to keep up his or her end of the mix-up. They are not cowards when it comes to defending themselves. They fight fast and have nothing but fighting in view. Man is their choice opponent. They make for his skull. Grizzlies under two years old fight only for liberty. Up to six years old, they fight to protect their young. When they get older, they fight to destroy an enemy. I mean when they are wounded or harried."

Ben Lilly considered that he knew more about bears than James Capen Adams, William H. Wright, or any other writer. "I sometimes feel," he said in a letter, "that I am not doing right by not giving my experiences [in written form] just as they come up."

He learned that grown grizzlies have a range about sixty-five miles across; black bears, about forty-five miles across. He discovered beyond all doubt that both bears and lions, likewise wolves, dogs and foxes, upon striking the trail of one of their kind can tell whether it has made a kill and has eaten; if so and if the new-comer is hungry, he or she will back-track the killer and eat on the remains of the carcass. He learned that his dogs could more easily trail a lion filled with fresh meat than one traveling empty. While he kept on one male lion's track for six days, his dogs treed and he shot three female lions that were, severally, back-trailing him.

Occasionally he trapped, especially for lions; but trapping is to trail-hunting as catching mud cats on a trotline in stagnant water is to fly-fishing for the gamiest of trout in a rushing mountain stream. He set traps not only at kills but on ground that he knew any passing lion would traverse. As a lure he favored cat-nip and devised a special way of preparing and placing it near a trap. He prescribed forty drops of oil of cat-nip to two ounces of crude oil, the smear to be sand-wiched between two pieces of cotton batting, this to be placed in an old perforated tin plate, the plate, with its sandwich, to be nailed against the blaze of a pine about three feet above the ground. Sap oozing from the blaze would, he said, seep through the holes in the tin and keep the cotton moist enough to preserve the catnip aroma for ten months.

From about 1912 to 1927, Ben Lilly lived the richest and most satisfying period of his life. In these times he never "came down" and holed up for the winter. He was out when the bears were in, for lions stay out the year around. After he had located a hunting range, he would establish a series of camps in natural shelters handy to water. The sign of these camps was wood he had dragged up. Sometimes he left jerked lion or bear meat. Jerky does not spoil. Occasionally he cured bear sides into "salt bacon." Now and then he hired a man to pack supplies into the mountains by mule; more often he carried them on his own back or on a burro.

One of the Arizona ranches he hunted on was the N O Bar, owned by Will Laney. Will Laney told me that Mr. Lilly would wear out a pair of shoe soles in two weeks. He generally resoled his own shoes, but before long the uppers would be snagged and worn away. Anybody he saw going to town could be sure of a commission to bring him a pair or two of hobnails. He would double-sole them, often plate the heels with burro shoes. After automobiles became common, he used cast-off tires for soling. A pair of his double-soled shoes that Mrs. H. B. Birmingham put on scales weighed just under twelve pounds. Yet wearing such shoes and carrying gun, dog chains and a pack of from 30 to 50 pounds, he could climb mountains all day. His rule for walking was: "Take it slow and steady. Put all your foot down, like a bear. Don't walk on your toes."

His equipment, typical of these Arizona-New Mexico years, consisted of a blowing horn, often used as a drinking cup at spring water; sometimes an old gramophone horn to aid his good ear in hearing the dogs bark; some light dog chains; the big Lilly knife for sticking and a smaller skinning knife; matches in waterproof tin; a sack of meal and a little sack of sugar; maybe some candy, too, for "the chillun" at a ranch that the signs might point to; sometimes rice; salt, though it could be dispensed with; a frying pan; a tin can for boiling meat and meal in, though often he did not encumber himself with any utensil, for on ranges he had worked over he had old lard buckets put away in scattered shelters; a stout ax with a full-length handle; extra cartridges in a tobacco sack, for he never wore a cartridge belt or loaded himself with much ammunition; a .30–30 rifle for lions and game meat;

a .33 caliber rifle if the quest was bear; in cold weather, sometimes a blanket and a piece of ducking. "The only time that pack bothers me is when I take it off," he said in 1914. "Then I feel so light that I want to float in the air."

He never used field glasses. Expecting to make only a short round, he might leave camp without supplies and then strike a hard-to-work trail that would lead him clear out of the country. From such a hunt he and his dogs would come in utterly spent. Then they would gorge and sleep and lie around until restored.

He usually preferred boiling his food to frying it — clean contrary to Old South tradition. He always tried to get freshly ground meal. His choice of frying fat was lion grease. Sometimes he cooked ash cakes. At his **G O S** camp, he would cook garden squash in season and make a custard of eggs and milk. He was a great milk drinker when milk was available. Occasionally he brewed imported Oriental tea; more often his tea was from piñon leaves, the leaves or bark of wild cherry, or some other native plant.

He had various ways of sleeping more or less warm. One way was to build a fire in a scooped-out place sheltered from the wind, then remove the coals and lie on the warmed ground. Another way was to gather pine needles into a sheltered place and to huddle down in them with his dogs. Sometimes he fired two parallel logs and lay between them. Once at least he set a big fallen tree trunk afire and slept on it until it got too hot.

"But a log is an awful hard bed, Mr. Lilly," one young hunter trying to keep up with him said.

"No harder'n me," was his reply.

"The Lilly fire," as he called it, was small, Indian style. Built in front of the right kind of rock shelter, it would, even in zero weather, warm the rocks and, by reflection, the man. One cold night in the mountains James K. Blair, who was hunting with Lilly, invited him to share a big bedroll.

"Lots of covering," Lilly observed.

"Yes, I believe in a warm bed," Blair said.

"All right, but I believe I'll take off one pair of pants and one shirt," and Mister Ben Lilly took them off.

When warm weather came, he shed outer clothes wherever he happened to be. Like the lard buckets, old clothes and shoes in an occasional rock shelter still tell that Ben Lilly passed that way.

In his camp headquarters he kept the Bible and a green-painted breadbox for holding his papers. A good part of the Bible was in his head, and he "could quote it like Leviticus himself." Generally he carried a pencil and tablet for diary entries.

[136]

Most hunters belonging to the mountains prospect on the side, or at least keep an eye out for signs of mineral. Nat Straw was always looking for the Lost Adams Diggings, Bear Moore for the silver ledge under a waterfall. The only sign Ben Lilly ever sought was the sign of the hunted; still he was not blind to the color of rocks.

At one time he kept an eye open for the Lost Dugout, supposed to be in a high and rough mountain on the Middle Fork of the Gila River — if it is not somewhere else. The story went that President Porfirio Diaz of Mexico, a short time before his downfall, sent a fortune in gold out of his country to be hidden for future recovery. The trustees hid the gold in a kind of dugout overlooking a canyon ample enough to swallow a half-dozen ordinary canyons and then fell out among themselves and killed each other to the last man.

One night a **G O S** cowboy failed to show up in camp. He came in next day admitting that he had got "kinder lost" and cut off by canyon curves while running a maverick cow. In running this cow he sighted, so he said, the Lost Dugout. Like two or three other men claiming to have seen it, he could not go back to it. An eccentric solitary named Santa Cruz Smith whom I ran into on the Gila and who had spent plenty of time looking for the Lost Dugout seemed resigned to his failure because Ben Lilly had also missed seeing the place.

John D. Gutherie of the Forest Service once asked another guard named Ulace Casto if he knew where Lilly was trapping, or if he had talked with him.

Ulace spoke very slowly and had a drawling speech. "Yes," he replied, "I seen him over on Bear Wallow last week. I didn't exactly talk to him, but I listened at him."

That talkativeness would peter out after the reserve of silence from months of solitude had been drained off. Fred Winn, who camped with Lilly many times, says that after talking a blue streak for a while at a fresh encounter, he might lapse into silence and not say a word for hours.

If he took a dislike to a man, or had an instinctive aversion to him at first sight, he would close up like a clam. A cold "Yas, suh, yas, suh" would be all the unliked man's talk drew out of him. His spirits rose at the prospect of consorting with friends, but it is to be doubted if he ever hungered for human association poignantly enough to turn aside from a hunting trail to seek it.

After his passion for sleeping in the open reached its zenith, he would sometimes refuse to spend the night in a cabin with a friend. "One November," Fred Winn recalls, "I got snowed up on a deer hunt and holed up, alone, in an abandoned cabin. About dark Ben Lilly and his dogs came along. He hadn't seen anybody in a long time and I was sure glad to see him. We had plenty of talk but at bedtime, in spite of the snowstorm, he persisted in sleeping outside with one blanket and his old piece of canvas." Sleeping indoors would give him pneumonia, he said. An old cowboy song goes, "You'll never catch consumption with sleeping on the ground."

Consistency was no more of a hobgoblin to him than to Emerson. In 1920 he went to visit his brother Joe and Mrs. Joe Lilly at Mineral Wells, Texas, where Joe was "taking the waters." Out of consideration for Brother Ben's zeal for sleeping in open air, they engaged a hotel room with windows on three sides. Before he went to bed in the room, he fastened down every window.

Curiosity about what was going on in the world never piqued him. He might read a magazine that somebody brought him. Again, he might not. He never requested a newspaper. The cry made by the first southward-flying sandhill cranes in the fall was more interesting to him than any dispatch from Washington or London. Most of his reading, by no means extended, on wild animals was in books that educated men working for the government had introduced to him. "Once he ventured the remark to me that he had 'little book larning,' in just those words," Fred Winn said. "Yet he frequently talked like a man of education; he was not given to picturesque expressions of the soil." Slang was as foreign to his purist nature as Greek.

In only one statement have I found that he ever mentioned or discussed sex. That statement is from a geologist named J. T. Janes of Pinos Altos, New Mexico, who says that while associating with him in the mountains for about fifty days and nights he found that Mr. Lilly believed "excessive cohabitation to be a detriment to the progress of intelligent people." In other words, Mr. Janes got no more of sex from Ben Lilly than anybody else got.

When, at rare intervals, he came into Reserve, Clifton, Alma, Magdalena, Silver City, Taos, or another of the far-apart towns of New Mexico and Arizona, he came with horn, hounds, rifle and ax. Standing, wondering and pleased, in the street, dressed like old Bill Williams, who thought that when he died his soul would transmigrate into the body of a bull elk, and looking out of his beard like God-consulting Moses, he was an object of curiosity to the populace.

The sense of wonder that kept the world fresh for him was nourished. He never stayed long enough in any town to wear out the novelty for himself or others.

He captured young lions and raised them — not because he was lonesome for pets, like dungeoned Peter Ellis Bean feeding flies to a lizard and making a companion of it, but because he wanted to observe the habits of lions. One day he observed a pet grown lion use a hind foot to rake up those little bars of twigs and leaves popularly called "lion markers." Like everybody else interested in the subject, he had supposed that the markers are made with the front feet. Here was a fact to delight him. He fed deer meat to these pet lions the year round.

In 1917, Bela Birmingham, now of Horse Springs, New Mexico, was ranching north of Reserve, near the Arizona line. Mountain lions were very numerous and destructive of livestock in that region. The superintendent of the Biological Survey had promised Birmingham that Ben Lilly would be over soon.

"Towards the first of December," Mr. Birmingham says, "my brother-in-law, Grover Mayberry, and I were gathering up our saddle horses to move them out of high country for the winter. Just after we rode into camp late on Saturday evening, hobbled our horses and were preparing to cook dinner and supper combined, we heard hounds trailing something up Largo Canyon. In about half an hour the dogs crossed the canyon not more than forty yards from camp and started back down it on the other side.

"We felt certain that the dogs must be Ben Lilly's and that they were after a lion. The trail sounded so hot that we expected to hear them barking 'treed' any minute. We grabbed our bridles, saddled up as fast as we could, put rifles in scabbards and were mounting when a man walked into view about seventy-five yards away. He was talking a blue streak. Neither of us had ever seen Mister Ben Lilly, but we had heard enough about him to know that the stranger could be nobody else. He was saying something about not wanting to disappoint us. Then, as he got a little nearer, he said that as it was Saturday and already past five o'clock, he was going to call his dogs in and wait till early Monday morning to take up the lion trail. 'I never hunt on Sundays,' he said in his mild, Christianlike voice. He began blowing his horn and calling to his dogs. There were six of them, and very soon they were obediently at his feet. He had a spotted bitch tied fast to his waist.

"While Mayberry and I unsaddled and turned our horses loose again, I remarked to him in a low voice that I did not think a hell of a lot of a man who would pull off a hot lion trail on Saturday afternoon to wait till Monday morning to take it up again. Throwing the hot Dutch ovens off the fire, we resumed our cooking. Mr. Lilly was chaining his dogs, each one separately, to saplings and all the time talking. Those dog chains, aside from his gun, seemed to be the chief part of his luggage.

"We had plenty of beef; so we gave Mr. Lilly a front quarter to feed his dogs. He said that neither they nor he had eaten anything for the last forty-eight hours. He had left Reserve with the intention of coming straight to my ranch but had gotten off after lions and killed five on the way. Having fed the dogs, he said that if we didn't mind he would 'nibble' on some sourdough biscuits left from breakfast. Nibbling, I later learned, was one of his strong points. One time while he stood and talked, he nibbled up a big loaf of lightbread a ranch woman had given him.

"By the time we had fried a big steak in a sixteen-inch Dutch oven, baked fresh bread, made gravy out of flour and water, stewed some dried peaches and boiled coffee, he had nibbled away six or seven of those big cold biscuits. He was merely building up strength to tackle the main meal. Seeing how things were going, I put on another big steak. Then after

I finished eating, I cooked a third one, still bigger. He 'ate for long range,' he said.

"About sunup Sunday morning, Mr. Lilly, barefooted and in nothing but his underwear, built up a big fire off to one side of camp. Then he walked to a pool below us, broke ice fully half an inch thick, and plunged in. He returned to his fire and rubbed himself briskly with his undershirt. On his legs and back were lumps as large as hen eggs, from exertion and strain in climbing the steep mountainsides I supposed. He always 'went under water,' he said, at least once a week.

"Mayberry and I spent the day in camp listening to Mr. Lilly talk. He read some letters from his daughters that he had got in Reserve. Along in the afternoon he strolled off and was gone about an hour and a half. When he came in, he announced that the Sunday rest had really gained him time on the lion he was running. I asked how he figured that. He replied that according to the lay of the country the lion would be due south of camp a couple of miles early next morning. Mayberry and I looked at each other but did not say anything.

"Early Monday morning after breakfast, Mr. Lilly said he would go south to a certain saddle he had noticed amid the breaks of Devil's Canyon and would pick up his lion's trail there. It would be fresh, he said. Mayberry and I wanted to catch three or four horses we had missed on Saturday and told him we would overtake him later in the morning. He had bagged two big male lions by the time we reached him. One of them, he assured us, was the lion his dogs had been trailing Saturday.

"Mr. Lilly said that before making the next move he wanted to examine Needle Peak for lion sign. I told Mayberry to go to camp, pack up and take our outfit in to the ranch and I would make a swing with Mr. Lilly. When we got to Needle Peak, I reached for my watch and did not have it. I remembered that I had looked at it at 9:45. Mr. Lilly never carried a watch. We figured it was about noon. Mr. Lilly said I had no doubt lost the watch in coming through some thick oak brush and that he would back-trail me and get it. He said I had just as well go on in to the ranch. He gave me his dog chains, ax and other baggage.

"Then he called his dog named Tippy. He talked to Tippy as though he were another person, told him what they had to do. He rubbed his hands over my horse's nostrils and then rubbed them over Tippy's nose. 'Now, Tippy,' he said, 'you are going to trail this horse.' He tied Tippy to his waist with a chain maybe ten feet long, gave the other dogs to under-

[145]

stand that they were not to follow but were to stay with me. Soon Tippy had the chain stretched out, pulling straight ahead on the trail. My route in to the ranch was roundabout, owing to the roughness of the country.

"When I got in, I found Mr. Lilly and Mayberry eating a late dinner. The watch was ticking away on a corner of the dining table. Mr. Lilly said he had not back-trailed me very far before he discovered it about three feet to the left of my horse's tracks. This was the beginning of an acquaintance that led us to know Ben V. Lilly for his true worth as both man and woodsman."

The hunting range that came nearer being home to him than any other was the Gila National Forest. From 1920 until he ceased to hunt, he had his headquarters on the **G O S** Ranch, in this area, though he often went off on long excursions to other ranges.

"I was hunting for a certain large male lion," he wrote. "I found his old track and judged he was due. I thought his route must be under a rock cliff not far off. I looked and his old track was there. It was late Saturday evening. I commenced gathering wood and piling it up under this rock. There was not room to keep more than two dogs and myself; so I prepared a place for the other two dogs near by. We slept through the night. It snowed all Sunday and Sunday night and was fearfully cold. I had no bedding and kept by the fire to stay alive. I got out at daylight Monday morning and found that the big lion had been within twelve feet of where I was lying. I had some of his mate's meat hanging in a tree. He had smelled that and passed on." Of course Mr. Lilly followed and killed.

He noticed the pad marks and the toe marks, both, of an animal. The imprint of the folds of the pad told him whether a bear was a grizzly or a black. At maturity lions and bears have a round, plump pad, he said. As age proceeds, the pad wears flat. The front feet of a grown female lion are a little rounder and neater than those of a male. She carries her young farther back in the body than any other wild animal. If she is heavy with kittens, the outside toe on each hind foot spreads out a little. These and many other minute observations made trails as clear to Ben Lilly as the printed description of a criminal to any F.B.I. agent.

Sign consists of more than tracks. It includes bodily excretions, hairs rubbed off on logs and left on bushes and in beds, the markers and kills made by lions, the scratches and bites on trees by bears, a log or rock turned over by an ant-hunting bear, the flattened grass where a lion has crawled on its belly to spring for a deer. To read sign aright, a hunter must know the lay of the land, its waterings, passes, hiding places, seasonal foods, topographical relation to other ranges favored or avoided by wild animals. He must be able to recognize not only what an animal has done but judge what it will do; he must know the instincts that direct its acts.

Ed Steele was losing stock to bears in the Escudilla Mountains. He had studied out all the bear runways and passes over the rough country around him and had set traps. The bears were not deterred. He sent for Ben Lilly. Upon arriving, Mr. Lilly asked him to spring all the traps, so that his dogs would not be endangered. He would not knowingly hunt in a country where other men were trapping. Then together, the two men climbed a peak that surveyed a great sweep of land.

"Mr. Lilly sat there for a good while looking out over the roughs," Ed Steele wrote me. "Then he stood up and began pointing out the different runways as they crossed certain creeks and ridges. Pointing to the northeast corner of the mountain below us, he said, 'Right there is the main cross-junction of all the bear trails in this section. Any bear coming into this part of the mountains, no matter whether he has ever been here or not, will pass right there. Now, down by that quaking aspen is a draw coming out of the mountain. That is a bear crossing.' He pointed to a spot where I always set a trap. Next he pointed to a ridge six or eight miles to the east and said, 'The bears use that ridge extensively in the summer.' They did.

"He knew lion the same way. If he found lion track too old for the dogs to make headway on, he would likely go to a good lookout point and stand there gazing out around the mountains; then he would take his dogs and go to a spot he had picked out four or five miles ahead. He had decided that the lion had crossed at that point. It generally had. If the trail at this place was still too cold to work, he'd pick out another place on ahead to cut across to, and so on until the smell got fresh enough for the dogs to follow."

About 1919, A. L. Inman, who had just entered the employ of the Biological Survey, was put with Ben Lilly to learn the techniques of predatory control. "After I had been with him only a day or two," Inman told me twenty-one years later, "we were following a lion when we struck a bear track. Mr. Lilly examined it and said that it had been made by a two-year-old male the night before. He pointed out a

CHAPTER VII

"That Taos Bear"

IN 1921, fourteen years after he had been "Chief Huntsman" to Roosevelt, Ben Lilly again withdrew from solitude to guide the most elaborately planned hunt the West has known since the Earl of Dunraven, led by Buffalo Bill and Texas Jack, bombarded the wapiti of the Yellowstone. It was enterprised by W. H. McFadden, Oklahoma oilman. For months before it started, promoter and sportsman Monroe H. Goode was spending his time and Mc-Fadden's money getting men, dogs and equipment together. The plan was to start on the Mexican border and hunt through the Rocky Mountains to Alaska.

Early in the spring four big wagons, each drawn by four big mules, set out north from Lordsburg, New Mexico. With the wagons was a train of pack mules, manned by professional packers, and enough horses and horsemen to drive a trail herd to Montana. The combined packs of dogs numbered forty-five, one dog alone having cost one thousand dollars. There were enough guns and ammunition to start a revolution in Nicaragua. A commercial photographer had been hired out of his studio to take pictures. The chief cook had a corps of helpers. The wagons held cases of maps, cases of Scotch, and provisions both delicate and substantial in proportion. Tents and servants assured comfort to ladies and gentlemen. The outfit had no time schedule, no limit on cost. Fresh supplies could be obtained at various points. Freehanded McFadden proposed to give his friends, in groups and in relays, an outing to remember. He would have to be absent from the expedition many times, but it was to go on just the same. Side hunts would be made east and west, wherever the signs pointed. For the first stretch of the hunt, through New Mexico, Ben Lilly was to be the main sign reader. His chief mission in life became to get McFadden a chance at a grizzly bear. Black bears and mountain lions were also on the program.

Coming down the Mimbres River in a light spring wagon one day, McFadden overtook his guide.

"I've been following a blue lion," Ben Lilly said.

"Blue, you say?"

"Yes, don't you want a blue lion? Here's the evidence." He took out of his pocket some blue hairs gathered from the under side of a crooked log on which the lion had rubbed his back. It was early June and lions were shedding.

"Well, get in the wagon and let's ride to camp," McFadden said.

"No, I'll get cold if I ride. I'll run ahead and open the gates." He had come nineteen miles that day and waded the Mimbres River eighteen times. He was going to camp to get his dogs, having been scouting without them.

The night turned out cold. McFadden insisted that the aging hunter sleep in a sleeping bag, near him. At two o'clock in the morning, Ben Lilly crawled out of it. "I'm choking to death," he said. "I'm going after the blue lion. Don't you want to go?"

"No."

"Then I'll see you in Silver City, and have the skull and hide."

This was Thursday morning. On Sunday morning Ben Lilly walked up to McFadden in Silver City, picking the flesh out of a skull with a knife, a fresh hide slung over his shoulder. "Here is the blue lion," he said.*

At night he would lie down in his blanket off to one side of the lighted, luxurious, tented camp. Often he boiled corn meal to eat instead of gorging on the pro-

* Not robin's-egg blue.

fuse dishes provided by McFadden's cooks. If he did
not leave before daylight to scout, he would be standing in blue denim awaiting emergence of shivering
sheepskin-coated guests. Their ways were all right
with him; his way of austere simplicity was the way
he wanted for himself.

On June 29 he struck the trail of a grizzly in mountains above Taos. He followed it for thirty hours without letup, and when he quit it to notify his patron, he
knew where the bear would be during the next thirty
hours. Just at this point McFadden had to leave for
the East on business. He left instructions for Lilly to
keep the bear located until he could return. The hunting party moved on. All the rest of the summer and
into the fall Ben Lilly shadowed the bear. He followed the wandering trail over northern New Mexico
and into Colorado. He came to ground still warm
from the grizzly's body, got left far behind. He sent
in reports:

"*Saturday, August 6th, 1921.* Going north for
Wheeler Peak in Colorado. I trailed him until dark.
It rained that night and next day. It rains from one to
three times every day. On Friday at 11 o'clock I found
his track again, headed for Wheeler Peak mountains.
I camped on his track. It come a big rain and hail that
evening. I took it up at daylight and followed it until

11 o'clock. A heavy rain put the track out. He was going south on the head of Pueblo River. I saw several small bear tracks while trailing him. He was feeding on berries and yellow jackets. He robbed about ten yellow jacket nests and followed after cattle tracks. . . .

"This big bear will have a range of 65 miles when disturbed and will change at any time. I am fully determined to work out his habits. It hurts me to let a bear rest that is wanted. . . .

"I found 22 old beds in one space of about 300 yards. That spot had been used by four different grizzlies — an old she, two two-year-olds, and this male. The other three bears have not used it for two years, but the big male used it this spring. . . .

"Spent 12 hours on 3 miles travel, picking my own route. If a bear had picked the route, I might have made only one mile a day. Whenever you want to see the roughest country, trail a grizzly. . . .

"I can tell a grizzly's claw mark a year after it has been made on a tree. I can tell the tooth marks. A Monster bear will not come back to a carcass to eat after he finds a man has been around. Other bear will come and eat. An old male will strike out for another range as soon as he gets filled up. Even if it is twelve months later, show me where one of these big fellows has left his sign, and in a few minutes I can tell you what happened. . . .

"A black bear that is fat and is living on good mast in his home range is easier killed than one that has just emigrated to a section where the feed is poor. When frightened, the fat bear will tree; the migratory bear is ready to keep on rambling from one bad place to another."

Clouds might prevent the "old male" from seeing his own shadow, but he could not run away from his shadower. Now he was in high rough places he had "been using for years," the shadower reported, "and no one knows of these places except me." That the big bear might not learn he was being shadowed, Lilly would not allow his dogs to run other bear in the country, and the only dog he used to follow this one was tied to his belt.

In late fall, Ahab suspended for a little while his wrath for the monster grizzly and came down to hear some word from his patron. No word. With "a hundred pounds on my back," he went up again. He was sixty-five years old now. This was in the Sangre de Cristo Mountains, in the Taos country. "We will never give that bear up. He has got to come — if I live. He can't get away. I know him too well to let him out, and he knows other people who are after him too well for them to get him. We will get him sooner or later — just as it suits you."

Now it was hibernation time. "My gun froze on the route. I didn't have a mouthful of meat for ten days." Mr. McFadden was on a luxury liner in the Atlantic Ocean, bound for Europe.

While the grizzly slept, Ben Lilly went to Taos to sit for the full-length portrait that his patron had commissioned Herbert Dunton to paint — "Buck" Dunton as his friends called him, "Dunton of Taos" as he magnificently signed his name. Grizzled hunters and grizzly bears were favorite subjects with Dunton. Lilly lived with him for twelve days, considered the portrait "true to life" — an opinion not shared by some — and reported that Dunton called it "the best piece he had ever done." In after times Dunton spoke of Ben Lilly's legs as his outstanding feature, along with his ability to read sign. In the spring the finished portrait, which is now in the New Orleans home of W. H. McFadden, was exhibited by the National Academy of Design in New York.

Ben Lilly was in Ponca City to get a string of McFadden dogs to take to Idaho, where the grand hunt had wintered. According to McFadden, he started from Ponca City on a train, but got out and walked and, upon arriving in Parma, Idaho, snow still on the ground, slept in the stockyards instead of going to the hotel where a room had been engaged for him. Idaho was the farthest north he ever hunted, though for years he yearned towards Alaskan bears.

He spent the summer of 1922 high up in the Rockies, attached to a camp that was frequently moved and that McFadden men but not McFadden himself dominated. His main object seems to have been to train his employer's dogs. According to his regularly kept diary, the dogs were lost a good part of the time. One of his own most cherished dogs got quilled by a porcupine and when finally found was blind and dying. One of his associates reported seeing a lion. "I am afraid he saw a coyote instead of a lion," Lilly mildly entered in the diary. He was mild also in entering the fact that target practice with pistols by a packer and a game warden confused the dogs and threw them off a hot bear trail. Once he rode a horse in order to keep company with a guest; then, just when he had a bear within reach, the guest insisted on fishing. The bountiful camp seemed to interest the campers more than hunting. He took "the grip." A dose of Epsom salts gave him a chill; two pills made him worse. They moved into a sheep country; a sheep got into a bear trap he had set. He dressed the sheep's wound and felt hopeful that it would recover, but "looked up the sheep herder and left a check for $5" to pay the owner for damages.

Frequent rains blotted out tracks, but between the last of May and the first of August Lilly observed the tracks of thirty-nine bears. He knew the age, sex and character of each trackmaker: "One four-year-old male," "one three-year-old male," a "two-year-old female," "one track grown-size but not plain enough to tell sex," "one small female yearling," "a barren she," and so on. On Big Pistol Creek he saw "hair rubbed on trees by a light cinnamon and a dark brown bear traveling eastward five days ago." From "bites in trees," he decided that a grizzly male had made two trips into that section the spring and summer of the preceding year, but had not been back. Without explanation, he entered in the diary for Sunday, October 15, 1922: "Lay over in camp. Helped skin the bear." On another Sunday he hunted by mistake, having lost account of the days, but rested from all labor on Monday. Altogether, it was not a satisfactory season. "Things" were in the saddle.

That fall he came back south, stopping in Denver, and, as arranged by McFadden's office, going to the Brown Palace Hotel. Wearing his blowing horn and followed by three hounds, his bearded figure was the cynosure of all eyes. He told a reporter for the *Denver*

Post, so the reporter said, that he wore the beard to keep mosquitoes off his face and the horn to call "the pups" in case they got lost in a train wreck or something like that. He did not think much of the backwoods language — manufactured in town — that the reporter made him speak. Trite, nonapprehending people often credited him with the vernacular that third-rate fictionists habitually put into the mouths of their rural characters. His mild protest recalls one made by Bigfoot Wallace to his biographer. "I know," Bigfoot said, "that my education is limited, but do give me credit for the little I have. People are not such fools as to think a man cannot be a good hunter or ranger, merely because he speaks his own language passably well."

He was glad to get back to the **G O S** range, where there were no camps to report to, no kennel dogs to interfere with his own, no voices to interrupt the silences. For years he continued to write McFadden letters about his dogs, the trails he had struck, the lions he had killed, the knives and pictures he was sending, the appropriateness of electing Mr. McFadden President of the United States — and "that Taos bear." "I will never feel right until we get him," he wrote, in April, 1925. That fall he was still "wild to get that bear." The final hunt was never made. Another rich man paid him $300 a month to tree lions for himself and his wife to shoot.

In these years of the 'twenties he virtually cleared the **G O S** and adjoining ranches of lions and bears. He was at the climax of enjoying his own prestige. He was a voluminous letter-writer and diary-keeper, but his diaries were scattered and lost. It seems to have been in 1924 that he began writing "my book." A California promoter encouraged him to imagine that a fortune-making film based on the proposed book would picture his hunting activities in the mountains. Like many people ignorant of the craftsmanship necessary for good writing, of the publishing business, and of the limitations of the book-buying public, he thought that a chronicle of his experiences and knowledge, once in book form, would bring a comfortable income "for the later years of life."

A mass-producer of Western fiction who came into the Silver City country sent him a note by a cowboy saying that he would be pleased to accompany him on a lion chase. After a good deal of trailing, the cowboy was able to deliver the note. Mr. Lilly read it slowly and then slowly penciled a courteous reply on a sheet of his pulp-paper tablet. He was after some stock-killers, he explained, and could not allow pleasure-hunters to interfere with business.

Royalties had made this Western writer acutely conscious of his own importance. Upon reading Ben Lilly's note, he turned to the cowboy bearer of it and blazed, "Apparently this old codger does not know who I am."

The cowboy shifted in his boots and grinned. "No, Mister," he remarked, "it ain't exactly that. You jest don't know who Ben Lilly is."

Everybody else knew. Over against Jerky Mountain, between the West Fork and the Middle Fork of the Gila River, a big "park" went — and still goes — by the name of Lilly Park. It is one of Mister Ben Lilly's tracks. He had already become a legend. People in town talked about the "big deposits" he had in banks, as well as about his checks written on aspen bark. In 1924 he had small amounts of money "laid up" in eleven or thirteen banks — he seemed unsure of the number — in El Paso, two Oklahoma banks, a bank or two in Arizona, and various New Mexico banks. Most of them closed when all the Western country went broke in the early 'twenties.

If a rancher or hunter anywhere in New Mexico or Arizona got to telling about some unusual experience he had had with a wild animal, he would likely add, "The first chance I get I want to ask Ben Lilly about that." Blunt Sloan ran a lion with dogs from

nine o'clock one morning until five that afternoon
before the lion treed. For a lion to stay ahead of running dogs that long is very unusual. When Blunt Sloan
finally met Ben Lilly up in the aspens Lilly strengthened reliance upon his knowledge by saying that he
did not know what possessed the lion but maybe he
was mad.

After Charlie Saucier, while freighting in the Black
Range, saw a grizzly standing on his hind legs slapping
a steer, both its jaws having been broken, and then
driving it off an open draw into timber, he consulted
Ben Lilly on bear tactics. "I never saw a bear hug,"
Ben Lilly told him. "All I've ever seen fighting
slapped."

Forest men concerned with the increase of porcupines, destructive to trees, consulted him. Yes, he
thought that the destruction of lions would result
in further increase of porcupines unless they were
otherwise checked. He had often observed the fondness of lions for porcupine meat. He always cut
open every animal he killed to learn about its diet.
Though he had never seen the act, he was convinced
that many lions knew how to roll a porcupine over
and claw the body open without getting seriously
quilled. Once he found a dead coyote with so many
quills in its head that he judged they had prevented

the coyote from eating and resulted in starvation.

Now and then he still sent specimens to the National Museum in Washington. How careful he was with the specimens is illustrated by an incident in which a young man named Edd Midgett took part. Late in 1923 Midgett was hunting on the Gila River, out from the famous Lyons Lodge, when he encountered Ben Lilly and "took up" with him. Stored carefully in a dry cave, the old hunter showed him the hides and skeletons of a female lion and two kittens, every bone minutely cleaned, to be shipped for mounting. One day the Lilly dogs struck the trail of a very old male lion. It leaped downward from a bluff into a piñon tree growing out obliquely into space 300 feet above the canyon floor. When a bullet from the Lilly .30-30 rifle took its life, the body lodged in a fork of the tree. Mr. Lilly had his ax, but to bring the lion carcass down by cutting the tree would mean crushed bones. This large, well-matured male was the very specimen to group with the female and the kittens already secured.

Mr. Lilly went to camp for two ropes and Old Smoky, his burro. He left Smoky on the canyon floor; then he scrambled ahead of the young man to the top of the bluff. Edd Midgett had climbed oil derricks. Now he swung down by rope from bluff to the base of the piñon, climbed its iced-over trunk, and fastened two ropes around the lion. He and Lilly managed to raise it to the bluff. The ground was covered with frozen snow. Ben Lilly sat down on it, tied one end of a rope around his waist, adjusted the lion's body carefully in his lap, and instructed Midgett to pull him down to Old Smoky. He turned himself into a sled to be dragged and braked over boulders rather than risk scraping a single hair from the lion hide. In camp the two men, as well as the dogs, had a feast on panther steaks.

How many panthers and how many bears Ben Lilly killed is not very important. To judge him on that basis is like judging the intellectual level of a newspaper by how much it weighs. The claim that Lilly killed "thousands" is foolish. One admiring — that is, gaping with uncritical wonder — fool * asserts that he averaged a lion a day while hunting. Actually, if he averaged one every two weeks he figured he was doing well. He had good runs, of course. "In 1914," he recorded, "I killed 9 mountain lions and 3 bears in one week." But this was a pocket, not a vein, as other statements from his diaries show: "I never struck a lion track from June 28th to the last of August, 1916. In another year I hunted all July and until the 25th of

* "For fools admire, but men of sense approve." — Pope.

August and struck only 3 lion trails and lost them on account of rains. In 1912, I killed 47 bears and lions, about an equal number of each; in 1913, I killed 48 bears and lions."

During one month of the spring of 1832, Davy Crockett of Tennessee, who went into some places ahead of the bees, killed, according to his autobiography, 47 bears, making a total of 105 for less than a year. In 1904, Ben Lilly told Ned Hollister that he had killed 105 bears in Louisiana and Mississippi during the preceding quarter of a century. Too many Crocketts had gone before for him to make a Crockett record. Yet he was far superior to Crockett in hunting skills, and as an observer of wild life Crockett had absolutely nothing to report. In the West, Ben Lilly became more of a lion man than a bear man. What he saw in the animals he hunted is of more consequence than the numbers he slew. It is to be doubted if during his whole lifetime of hunting he killed more than a thousand bears and lions put together. Considering his time, this was an enormous toll.

The records of the Biological Survey show, according to Dorr H. Green, Chief of the Division of Predator and Rodent Control, that B. V. Lilly "took" predatory animals as follows during his intermittent terms of employment with the Biological Survey:

October–December, 1916, 9 mountain lions; October–December, 1917, 8 mountain lions; February–December, 1918, 25 mountain lions, 8 bears, 2 bobcats; January–May, 1919, 7 mountain lions; October–November, 1919, 2 mountain lions, 1 bear, 1 coyote; June 1–August 14, 1920, 4 mountain lions, 3 bears. He was killing too many bears; "services were terminated." At times during his employment with the Biological Survey, B. V. Lilly would be sent to some very difficult region to get some particularly elusive and destructive predator. During twenty-six and a half months of the years 1916–1920 that he worked for the Biological Survey, he reported the destruction of only 55 lions and 12 bears. It is doubtful if, during the remaining time of this period, he more than equaled that number.

In his "Mountain Lion Record for 1922," he tells of killing 10 lions between June 14 and September 26 and adds that his total over a period of years for the Alma (New Mexico) section, which included the Blue River country of Arizona, was 109 lions. His biggest kills, as deduced from the articles he published in the *Producer*, were 47 lions and bears (about equally divided) in 1912, in the Alma district; 48 lions and bears in 1913, in the same Arizona-New Mexico range; 1914 and 1915, also "good killing"; 42 lions on the

G O S and Diamond Bar ranches during 4 months of 1919, after which the animals were much scarcer everywhere that he hunted.

In March, 1919, an article in the *American Magazine* reported that "during the past four years, in the Apache Forest Reserve alone, Lilly has tracked to death 154 lions, with 46 bears picked up on the side." Four years later, Fred Winn of the Forest Service, who knew Lilly very well indeed, reported that he had "disposed of over 400 mountain lions in Arizona, New Mexico and Texas." In 1943, Dr. A. K. Fisher of the Biological Survey wrote to Monroe Goode: "As I understand it, Lilly gave me his 500th lion, a fine male killed 30 miles north of the G O S Ranch, March 14, 1921. He very likely killed 50 to 75 after that, but of course this is a guess only." About the same time, E. E. Lee, noted Arizona hunter, wrote to Monroe Goode: "In the spring of 1925, Lilly told me he had just killed his 547th lion since 1912 — 'after they had begun to get scarce.' " On December 9, 1934, an article in the *Sunday Star* of Washington, D. C., evidently based on an interview with Ben Lilly, was entitled "Old Chap Has Killed 600 Lions." By this date the "old chap" had virtually ceased to hunt.

The Boones and the Crocketts skimmed the cream; Ben Lilly scooped up every drop of splattered milk from the cracks. In the letter of self-appraisal that he wrote Dr. J. B. Drake, in 1928, he said: "No other man will work as close as I have worked. I have worked in localities where not enough food could be carried to keep three men alive. I have worked where no water was to be had for 76 hours. In order to get to the animals I wanted, I went without food and water for days. I have stayed in snow from 3 to 12 feet deep for three weeks at a time and not even a blanket and I succeeded. I have followed a big grizzly for three days at a time, snow from 3 to 12 feet deep, never had a coat on, I killed him, and then I eat his meat. No other man will take such risks alone — not even a dozen other men together. I have killed the largest and best tribes of animals. I have hunted them so close that it would take longer for 100 of them to accumulate again than it took me to kill 1000."

No, numbers are not the index to Ben Lilly's career as a hunter.

CHAPTER VIII

The Lilly Dogs

IT is doubtful whether Ben Lilly could have recalled his first dog. Sometimes he had only a few dogs, sometimes many; he nearly always had two or three upon which he could rely to the utmost. They were of no undiluted breed. He was stronger on intelligence in a dog than on breeding for nose, ears, color, or anything else. His were Lilly dogs, just as his knife was the Lilly knife. The kind of dogs that had served him so well in swamp and canebrake led him through the roughest mountains of the West. The strain was predominantly pot-licker. In the mountains he wanted dogs with short ears and round feet, for the toes that go with long ears wear tender on rocks. He had little use for Airedales. He claimed they were not a distinct breed and therefore had no distinct interest; that following a bear, they would stop to chase a chipmunk; and that they would not give tongue on a trail or even after they treed. He was very jealous of the Lilly strain. During his big years as a hunter in the West, he would not sell a male without castrating him or a bitch without spaying her. His dogs wore collars of his own making, his name on the plates.

He knew how to make dogs do his will, felt kindly towards those doing it, would keep no others. He slept with them in zero weather, fed them when he could, and expected them to endure privation as well as he did himself. When a rancher at Pinos Altos, New Mexico, sent him a hurry call, in 1925, to run down a lion that was killing his cattle, Ben Lilly violated his custom of hunting afoot through the country to get to any place and took "the stage." The motion of the battered old touring car made him sick, but immediately after it halted at Pinos Altos he led his dogs straight to water. Then he went into the Watson store, which everybody who goes to Pinos Altos enters, and got a glass of water for himself.

An unkind wit might say that he justified the philosophy of the Kentucky sheriff in O. Henry's "The Theory and the Hound." "I never yet saw a man," the Kentucky sheriff said, "that was overfond of horses and dogs but what was cruel to women." But Ben Lilly was not fond of horses at all, and he was pitilessly discriminating towards dogs. If he got hold of a dog irresponsive to training, he would kill it. He would not give away a dog to be pampered in town. He thought that dogs had a right, like himself, to follow the instinct for hunting. A dog without that instinct was to him a betrayer of the species. If, after he had trained a dog, it persisted in quitting the trail of a lion or bear for something else — all else being trivial and irrelevant — he would call his dogs around him as witnesses, explain to them very definitely the crime of interfering with the work of good dogs and call upon them as fellow hunters to see justice in the death penalty. He would talk to the guilty one sternly but without anger, and then either beat him to death or shoot him.

One year on the **G O S** Ranch his pack numbered twenty-two dogs. He paid Mrs. John Mathews, wife of the ranch foreman, fifteen dollars a month to cook for them. In the course of years ferocious animals killed many of his dogs. He would take from three to five with him on a hunt, bring them in with sore and bleeding feet, and take out another string. He always had a young one along to train with the older dogs. He trained many dogs to trail by keeping them tied to his belt.

He gave training — the Lilly training — utmost credit for the superiority of his dogs as hunters. He said that a cur could smell as well as a hound and that if a man spent long enough time training a cur he might get a good trailer. He was too practical a hunter, however, to waste time trying to make a silk purse out of a sow's ear. He used curs for close fighting.

One day A. L. Inman noticed boys at the **G O S** Ranch running jack rabbits with Mr. Lilly's dogs and spoke to him about the matter, for no orthodox hunter allows his dogs to be spoiled in that way. "Oh," Mr. Lilly said, "when those dogs are with me, they won't even notice a jack rabbit."

To suppose that wet weather is more favorable for trailing than dry weather is a mistake, he said. "If it rains and then stays damp, good; but if the sun comes out on wet tracks, the scent is dried up, evaporates." Some dogs, he noticed, trail alongside tracks, rather than in them, scenting, it would seem, an odor blown off the animal and left on the ground.

He set to working out the first trail his dogs struck, no matter how old, provided it was workable at all, and no matter how good the chances of striking a fresher trail farther on. If a fresh trail crossed the old one, he could switch to it. If an old trail became difficult to work on a barren, hot, south mountain slope, he would cut over to the cooler, better-wooded north slope, where dampness and vegetation held the scent and the trail would freshen. If a lion trail was very

[173]

old, he'd say, "We'll gain when this fellow stops to kill."

He often talked about the wonderful trailers and hunters he had had. "Crook died the second Tuesday of February, 1925," he wrote in a letter two months after the event. "There seemed to be something stuck in his throat. He had a record of 437 lions and 213 bears. [These figures are out of reason; it is easy to make mistakes in figures.] I never owned a better dog. Five days before he died he trailed a lion that had been gone 8 days. One time he struck a bear track 7 days old and denned the bear." Crook's owner was elated at observing how the old dog's grandchildren could pick up a trail four or five days old. He was offered $500 for one of them named Frank but would not take less than $1000.

Crook was the last of a great pack distinguished also by Queenie, Jack, and Tippy, or Tip. Of the four, Tip was his favorite. He was one of a litter of nine whose mother had been in at a lion kill the day before she pupped. Hunting with other dogs, no matter how good, Mr. Lilly always depended on Tip for the final word. Tip was rather lazy and independent, but would wake up when he saw another dog switching his tail and smelling. "Let's wait and see what Tip says," would be Mr. Lilly's judgment. If, after investigating, Tip became indifferent, he would say, "Oh, it's just a wildcat or coyote or something like that." He often remarked, "It's a cash proposition with Tip, like me." When approaching a ranch, Tip would pick up energy and go ahead to explore for food. After trailing down many a lion and many a bear, he was killed by a grizzly. His master gave him a Christian burial on the topmost peak of Spring Mountain, in the Black Range. Later he went back and got Tip's skull, thinking it might, like a cast of Napoleon's head, have scientific value.

When a hunter bragged that his dogs never took a back-trail, Mr. Lilly would say, "My dogs take the back-track sometimes. It seems that the back-track is easier to follow sometimes." *

* "While there is no yardstick by which to measure the keenness of a hound's scent, there is, however, a way in which to get an approximate idea. When a hound approaches the trail of a man at right angles and scents his trail in the air, how does he know whether the man went to the right or the left? [He does not look at the tracks, does not know toe mark from heel mark.] Usually, he takes the right end of the trail; that is, the way the man went, the other way being called his back-trail. But sometimes, due probably to the wind or some other atmospheric condition, the hound is not sure which way to go and he will run some twenty yards in each direction alternately several times until he has fully made up his mind which is the right end of the trail to take. In my experience he is invariably right. The question, therefore, arises: How much difference is there in the strength of the scent twenty yards one side or the other of a given point? That difference is the measure of the keenness of a hound's scent." — Montague Stevens, *Meet Mr. Grizzly*, The University of New Mexico Press, Albu-

Mr. Lilly told me that one time he found his dogs after they had been alone with a lion for eight days. They had been barking so long, he said, that when he finally got within hearing distance he could not recognize their voices. During the eight days, as the trail plainly told him, they had quit the lion several times to go to water and to eat off a lion kill, a deer carcass, they knew about. Returning as they invariably and promptly did, and finding that the lion had jumped out, they would take his trail and run him into another tree. Generally, however, if no one came to his dogs within a reasonable time, they relayed each other, so that while one or two went for water, perhaps food also, at least one kept the quarry bayed.

The usual pack of dogs comes in, unless someone goes to them, before the night is over. The Lilly dogs understood it to be their business to stay with their quarry until the master found them. There was nothing miraculous about this. Joe M. Evans, of El Paso, recalls that one time while all the men were gone from their ranch in the Davis Mountains, the "womenfolks"

---

querque, New Mexico, 1943, page 81. Quoted by kind permission of the publishers.

Meet Mr. Grizzly has more acute observations on the nature of dogs than any other book I have read. The author was a New Mexico rancher with the perspective characteristic of minds trained at Trinity College, Cambridge.

noticed that the two ranch hounds kept coming in, one at a time, for food. They were evidently relaying each other. On the ninth day of this procedure a man who happened by the ranch followed one of the hounds after he had come in for a meal and found a lion in a tree, guarded there by the other hound. He killed the lion, little more than skin and bones.

Ben Lilly always wanted to know what was going on in the wild animal and livestock world, and his dogs were trained to lead him to any carcass — deer, calf, colt, cow or other animal — whether killed by a predator or not. His dogs were trained to expect a full meal from whatever they caught. They did not run deer. He claimed that feeding them upon the flesh of a varmint brought to bay made them more eager for the next chase, and he thought that his sharing lion and bear meat with them strengthened their attachment to him.

To him every good dog had a distinct personality. His description of Lilly, a hound that his friend W. H. McFadden named for him, will illustrate. "She was a true type of bright red fox hound, very trim, a fine trailer, with a beautiful voice that she used continuously, either trailing or running. She had scars made by bear. Her appearance would have made any hunter proud of her. She was perfect as a hound and she ranked with mixed blooded dogs for speed and with Airedales or other terriers for grit. She would run all day alone or in a pack."

To watch his dogs work was a lively pleasure to him. They had an understanding with each other that was both personal and technical. In a long letter to W. H. McFadden, written in 1923, he detailed their trailing techniques and accomplishments with a kind of solemn glee, a pride transcending any egoism, and the plain dignity that belongs only to elemental life.

"At eight o'clock a man came to me and told me that the morning before he run a lion off a calf killed about daylight. I paid him to take me and the 3 dogs to the calf in a car. We stopped some distance away and left the dogs in the car while we went to examine the calf. First thing I noticed tracks of two lions instead of one. I trailed them for 25 or 30 steps. I says, 'A male and a female.' They left going northward, traveling about 60 yards apart. We went back for the dogs. Crook and Monk raised their heads when they got in 50 yards of the tracks and began to bark. I asked the man to hold my guide dog, named Hunt, until I started them. I showed Crook one track, then put Monk on the other. I went back and got Hunt and took out. Inside of a half hour, the lions crossed over each other's tracks three times. They were hard to trail and both dogs would lose. I saw it happen. When Monk or Crook lost, he would go right on working to pick the trail up again while the other was barking on the trail that belonged to him. When they lost together at a place where the lions crossed, each worked till he picked up the right track again. Neither one paid any attention to the lion the other was trailing. It was dusty and dry. I could see the tracks of each lion plain and each dog kept the track he started with.

"They went up some very high bluffs and kept getting faster and faster. By noon the mountain sides were very hot. My guide dog got so hot I couldn't hear nothing but his panting. He decided that he couldn't hear and that I knew it all, and any direction I looked he would want to lead me. So the hunting dogs got away from me. I searched in all directions and finally I thought I heard them both barking treed, but wasn't certain. The guide dog thought they were north. I went in that direction but couldn't find no track and circled back east to where I had thought I heard them. Finally I did hear Crook barking treed. He had the female lion. I shot her through the heart, but she jumped so high and so far out from the tree I was afraid I had just creased her and fired on her again as she jumped. She was dead when she hit the ground, I guess. I drug her out, tied the guide dog, and walked off about 400 yards in a direction I hadn't been in and heard Monk barking treed somewhere.

"I went back and took the entrails out of the dead lion and hung her up in a tree and with Crook and the guide dog went to the spot where I had heard Monk. After we waited about a minute, he barked treed again. We all three differed as to where he was. I thought he was one way; Crook wanted to go his way. I tied him to me with the guide dog and took Hunt's advice. I ran about two hundred yards before stopping to listen. Nothing sounding. I kinda began to reason and said, 'If Monk is on the other mountain, I could have heard him from the dead lion. Hunt is wrong.' I went back north, upgrade, checking up as I went and before long heard Monk barking regular. All three of us agreed now. Monk had the male lion in a spruce growing along a bluff. I shot him in one shoulder so as to have a little race. When he jumped, those dogs went over the bluff. They caught him and it was a very interesting fight.

"The lions had left the calf 30 hours before I started the dogs. Within two hours I killed both. While trailing, I saw the track of a third lion. It was old but workable. The next morning I put the dogs on it. While they were trailing, they struck tracks of a female bear and cub. I left Monk to trail the bear southwest and fol-

sound detector — a boy keen of hearing and fast of legs. Tutt said, "I found him a coal-black boy with long legs that was a fine walker. When Mr. Lilly came back from the hunt, he says, 'Tutt, that boy is a good walker and he can hear good, but he hears better in the direction the dogs are running from than in the direction they are running to.'" In other words, the boy was afraid of bears. After that experience, Ben Lilly preferred dog over man for guide. A good guide dog left him free to observe tracks and other signs.

Once he got a little too much of associating exclusively with his dogs. For three months, as he told the story, he had been hunting in the great woods without seeing a human being or hearing a human voice. One day he was sitting by his campfire, deep in reverie, his dogs haunched about, half asleep and dreaming. Suddenly a little dog that seemed to be dreaming especially hard lost its balance and fell against a big dog in such a way as to knock him over. The big dog awoke with indignation boiling, jumped on the little dog, and in a minute the whole pack was yelping and fighting. The little dog's fall, the big dog's resentment and then the uproar struck Ben Lilly as being so funny that he laughed out loud. The sound shocked him, the sound of a human voice, his own. He decided he must be bordering on insanity if he was so affected by a man's voice. He broke camp and came in, for a while, to people.

Wherever he went, throughout his lifetime, he met people who were fond of him. He was no pariah, but he was never intimate with any man. It is doubtful whether he was ever intimate, beyond physical contact, with any woman. If he had any intimacy of feeling towards another creature, it was towards John, the dog of Louisiana days that he remembered with most warmth, or Tippy, or Crook.

CHAPTER IX

Ben Lilly on Panthers

"IF you follow a lion four or five days and don't get some education," Ben Lilly said, "you had better go back to plowing."

This chapter is taken mainly from Ben Lilly's manuscript described at the beginning of the book, his diary of 1916, *Mountain Lion Record*, and a few notes that I made after talking with him. He wrote wanderingly, instead of logically grouping facts on any particular phase of the subject, and as he composed sporadically without reviewing what he had set down, his composition is filled with repetitions. The matter that follows is his, but arrangement and considerable punctuation are mine.

Anybody who will comb the homely narratives of pioneer people made during the eighteenth and nineteenth centuries, especially as pertains to the South, will meet many accounts of attacks by panthers on human beings — not all of them authenticated and yet not all mere folklore. *Quadrupeds of North America* by John

James Audubon and John Bachman contains several
vivid instances drawn from the general region in which
Ben Lilly's stories of panther attacks are laid. We may
rest assured that in telling these stories he added virtually nothing to what he had heard. His memory for de-
tail was precise. He made the common error of ascrib-
ing moral attributes to animals — bravery to the grizzly,
loyalty to the timber wolf, cowardice to the mountain lion; however, except in telling bear stories to
children, he seems never to have personalized animals.

In old age, Ben Lilly had a gentle nature, but his
gentleness was more moralistic than aesthetic. His inclination to the mystical did not find in the panther

> A pard-like spirit, beautiful and swift.

He never questioned:

> Tiger, tiger, burning bright
> In the forests of the night,
> What immortal hand or eye
> Could frame thy fearful symmetry?

His blood never curdled at imagining the panther's
scream that he had never heard. He had seeing eyes,
and, whatever the fare of his camp, it was always the
"bread of truth and sincerity." Let him say:

[185]

I grew up in Mississippi and Louisiana hearing the American puma called pantha [panther]; in Mexico I heard it called *león* [lion], also *pantera;* in Idaho I heard it called cougar; in New Mexico and Arizona it is generally lion or mountain lion. Under these names I have killed the same animal, measurements varying little, from the Mississippi River to the Continental Divide. My main experience with panthers has been in New Mexico.

Correct measurements of wild animals can be made only before they are skinned, and then the figures must be written down or they will be confused in memory. Measure the animal from nose to tip of tail for length, also measure the tail separately; for height, measure from the bottom of the front foot to the top of the shoulder and from the bottom of the hind foot to the top of the hip. The fresh hide of a full-grown male lion will stretch about three feet; thus the size of many lions has been stretched. While collecting specimens to send to the Biological Survey in Washington, D. C., I heard that a lion killed in Texas measured 13 feet. I had sent in a big fellow from Mexico that measured 8 feet, 9½ inches, and I wanted one of the large Texas specimens if it could be obtained. I sought out the man reported to have measured the 13-foot lion. He was a carpenter. He said: "I wrote down the measurements. I will get the book." He got the book. It read "7 feet long." I did not hunt farther for a 13-foot Texas lion. Grown males in New Mexico average from 7 to 7½ feet in length; grown females, from 6 feet, 3 inches to 6 feet, 8 inches; one female measured 7 feet, 5 inches.

Lion kittens, which are about the size of rats when born, are spotted with black-yellowish spots over the face, back, sides and the front part of their legs. Their eyes, which open about nine days after birth, are deep blue. They grow very fast and at the age of from four to seven months shed their original hair, losing the spots and turning to the adult color. At the same time they shed their milk teeth and grow permanent ones. If they are fat and thrifty, they shed early; if they are under-nourished or are kept in close quarters, they shed slow and late. The shade of lion color varies somewhat with altitude and other conditions. A fat female in mountain country that travels by day in search of food will be a shade lighter in color than a fat female of the same mountains that lays up in the shade all day and hunts only at night.

Usually the first litter that a female brings consists of two kittens; thereafter, the litter averages three kittens. Occasionally four kittens are born; I once took five from a bed. Now and then the first bearing

[187]

is of a solitary kitten; I killed one very old female carrying only one kitten. I have found kittens born or about to be born in every month of the year. Females often raise two sets of kittens within a period of from twelve to fifteen months.

While the kittens are helpless, the mother usually stays with them all night, doing most of her hunting between three P.M. and a little while after dark. About two weeks before the little ones are born, the female becomes especially active in killing. She drags carcasses into thick underbrush or among rocks or next to a shaded log, covers them with leaves, bark, dirt and other trash, and prepares beds within a mile or so of the kills. She has food ready so that she can eat for a while without hunting much and stay close with her young, supplying them with milk. After leaving them, she comes back over a route different from the one she took going out. A bear comes back to her cubs the same way she went out.

After the kittens are three or four months old, she leads them to her kills so that they can eat. Young lions drink lots of water; older ones, very little; a female giving milk drinks more water than any other grown lion. The female with active kittens tries to make kills convenient to water. She hides her young in the securest places. She may rove off up to seven miles in search of prey. While she is gone, the developing kittens may go to water alone or eat off some kill to which she has already led them.

With one hound tied to my belt and another one working loose, I have trailed many lion families not only to catch them but to find out what they were doing. In the snow I have seen where one of three kittens followed its mother while the other two branched off, coming back to her farther on. One family I followed went eight miles with only one stop. The lioness lay down under some rocks; the kittens sucked and played all around her. When I killed her I saw that she was giving plenty of milk. She was leading her three young ones to the carcasses of two sheep she had killed. I have known a lioness to lead her kittens to a carcass, leave them there, go on, make another kill, cover it up without taking a mouthful of flesh, and then go on to a carcass she had left five or ten days before and make a meal off it.

In every litter of kittens I have found there were both male and female, never all of one sex. At birth the male is a little larger than the female. As soon as the kittens are old enough to nose around, the male will have a little braver motion than the female, and she will incline to be a little crosser and more cautious. The little ones will be up early in the morning, noticing any movement in the sky and trees and on the ground. The fluttering of a bird in a bush makes them react as if to catch it. They will try to catch anything comparable to their size. They are natural hunters, and if left orphans after they are able to move about, they no doubt catch frogs, lizards and grasshoppers and thus exist, like coyote pups. I once followed three half-grown kittens for three days before killing them near a two-months-old calf they had ganged up on and brought down. During those three days they ate nothing.

A grown lion hunts and kills alone. The young ones have the pack instinct. By the time they are eight or ten months old, they are active killers of fawns and young stock. At this period, the mother lion eats from their kills, although still killing for them. When they are from nine to eleven months old, she leaves them, preparatory to bearing another litter. Should she lose her second batch of kittens, she will at times rejoin the yearlings. Often a mother lion with kittens in a nearby bed will eat on a carcass with her yearlings. I have seen where the yearlings had visited the kittens.

Few people have worked out the roving habits of mountain lions. By the time a family is grown, their mother has shown them a lot of country. The young male strikes out earlier for himself than the young female, and he goes farther. Some females go a long way, but adult males are generally the farthest rovers. After an adult lion makes a kill, it eats maybe two or three times over a period of three or four days, drinking water and lying within reach of the kill until ready to rove. Then it travels on an empty stomach. The next time it is hungry, it usually makes a fresh kill instead of returning to the old one. The traveler is often seeking other lions. One male lion I trailed met a female twelve miles from where he had killed a young steer and led her back to the carcass.

At some places where he finds leaves or straw on the ground, especially pine needles, the male stops and with a hind foot makes two parallel strokes from eight to ten inches long and about seven inches apart. If the leaves and straw are deep, they will be mounded up three inches or so between the strokes at the rear. These "lion markers" are made only on a full belly. They tell other lions about the one that has passed and about the food he has left. In fifteen miles of travel a lion makes a dozen or so markers. While hunting food he seldom makes one, only while hunting other lions. Normally he makes a round about every fourteen days. On returning to the vicinity of a marker he has left, he inspects it, unless he is hunting food, to see if another lion has been there, and often he makes a second marker within two or three feet of the first. Any visiting male from four months old up will paw in the marker; that is the only sign he leaves. Females seldom paw. Nearly all lions of both sexes prefer traveling over an established route and are more or less regular in making a beat, provided they or the animals they live on are not disturbed. This route is in the roughest mountains, especially along the tops of bluffs.

Availability of food determines many of the movements of all wild animals, but individuals vary greatly in both traveling and killing. At times a lion will stay in one locality for several weeks, making all its kills within a radius of a few miles; then this lion will strike out on a trip that takes several days to make and not return to the home grounds for weeks and even months. An old male may make his kills twenty miles apart. A female with young sometimes kills two or three animals in a night, if she finds prey convenient.

Like other wild things, lions have a tendency to rove in the spring and again in the fall. Some individuals seem kin to the gypsies. In November, 1912, while I was trailing six days behind a grizzly, I saw a female lion's track that was about eight days old. The left front foot of this lion made a five-toed track; she had, I judge, been caught in a trap that pulled one toe out of joint in such a way that it printed two points on the ground. She was being followed by two yearlings. This was in the Blue River country of eastern Arizona. I kept on the trail of the grizzly and found where he had struck the trail of a male lion. He detected that the lion was leaving a kill and he back-tracked the lion to the carcass of a large buck, which he finished devouring. On Sunday, while I was resting on this grizzly's trail, a heavy snow fell, blotting out all sign, and so I did not get to follow him or the lions farther.

Two years later, I saw the five-toed lioness track again, thirty miles south of where I first saw it. Two yearlings were again following her. The tracks were three or four days ahead of me. For about thirty miles I followed them south. During that stretch of travel the three lions did not stop. Then a big snow covered up all sign. I was hunting over a wide country, and during the next two years I inquired of all hunters and trappers I met concerning the five-toed lioness. Nobody knew anything about her.

In 1916, four years after I became acquainted with the five-toed track, I met it again south of Reserve, New Mexico, a full hundred miles from where I first saw it. It was pointed in the direction of the original range. It was fresh, and after following it all afternoon

I killed the maker of it about sundown. That night a man and his son were in camp with me, and while we sat by the fire he asked me how far a lion travels. My answer was, "As far as the ranges suit it." A long drouth, a long spell of snow, a plague of insects, or some other natural factor will cause lions and other wild animals to migrate.

The day after I killed this lion I took her back-track to learn whether she was hunting or just traveling. When I killed her, her stomach was empty and there was a scrape on her side that appeared to have been made by a buck's horn. I thought that she might have killed a deer and that then, before she could eat, a stronger lion might have driven her away. If so, I was going after this stronger lion. After back-trailing about six miles I found where she had leaped on a very heavy buck. He had plunged about in a low, thick, rough, scrubby thicket while she hung to him. Both of them had lost a lot of hair. Judging from all the signs, the buck had dislodged her by dashing her against especially thick brush. The brush through which he bounded away was too thick to allow the lion to stay on his back. He must have hooked her after he dislodged her. I judged she had raised kittens that season but had lost them. It would be hard to say where that female lion had been during the four years that passed between my first seeing her track in Arizona and then killing her a full hundred miles away in New Mexico.

The lion is tasty. When he can, he kills the choicest and fattest, though crippled and sick deer that cannot get away fall victims. In a lion country it is the fittest of game animals that survive and breed. Lions habitually rip the entrails out of whatever they kill before covering it up. This keeps the carcass from quickly spoiling. In warm weather lions of all ages and of both sexes try to place their kills in cool, shady places where the meat will keep better. Sometimes they drag and carry a carcass a long way. In warm weather, however, a high percentage of their kills spoil and get eaten up by coyotes, wildcats, buzzards and other carrion eaters. In hard-freezing weather, lions like warm meat. Even when they are hungry, they will at times pass by a frozen carcass that is perfectly fresh, perhaps covered with snow, and go on until they make a kill. If the meat is not spoiled, a lion will sometimes return to a kill up to fifteen days old.

I think that a grown lion will average killing two animals the size of a deer every ten days, say seventy animals a year.* All lions seem to be especially fond of

* "A deer a month would be closer to the mark," scientific investigators of New Mexico concluded. (*A Preliminary Survey of the Mountain Lion*, University of New Mexico Press, Albuquerque, 1939.) Victor H. Cahalane (*Mammals of North America*) upholds

colt meat. Whenever horse stock is within reach, they prey on it. They generally prefer venison to beef. I have found the meat of porcupine, grouse, cottontail rabbit, skunk, burro, mule, horse, deer, cattle, goat, sheep and hog in lion stomachs.

Carnivorous animals want green grass or other fresh vegetation after eating meat. At times when green grass was not available, I have found dead grass in the stomachs of lions, wolves, coyotes, foxes and bobcats. The mother of lion kittens often leads them to cliffs that drip water and grow tender vegetation even during drouth and cold weather. Sometimes a lion will swallow a sprig of fresh vegetation that the stomach can't retain; yet the system craves it, needs it. It is said to be hard to keep a domestic cat on a steamboat. I have talked to steamboat engineers on this subject and they said that no cat thrives long on a boat. The theory is that cats can't get grass aboard, though they have all the food they want. I would like to know if

---

the idea, shared by many other biologists, that the mountain lion's toll of deer is "frequently more beneficial than harmful" to the species. Examination of eleven carcasses of deer killed by lions in New Mexico, he says, showed abnormality in each. The lion is "tasty" all right and no doubt prefers his venison fat and tender, but in lion and coyote country it is the sick and crippled deer that succumb first, leaving the strong, the alert and the beautiful to breed. In some parts of the hill country of central Texas cleared of all predatory animals the deer have within the last twenty-five years or so noticeably decreased in size.

a cat living on a boat ever reached the age of twelve years.

I have raised several lions and bears and have learned from experience that in order to thrive they require room to exercise in and something green now and then as much as they need meat. Few wild animals in captivity get enough exercise or enough pure air. Lion kittens raise better if taken immediately after birth, before they learn to know their mothers.

Every kind of animal I have hunted eats in one zone something not available in other zones. Climate and soil make the differences. In Mexico and New Mexico, and the West in general, you seldom hear of a mountain lion attack on man. Here, fat cattle, horses, deer and sheep are nearly always available. In the lower Mississippi River country where I grew up, stories of attacks by the panther were common. Most of the stories, though not all, were of a long time ago. In early days in the South, panthers did not have the choice of food that those of the West have. The first settlers in the low, hot lands often owned only a dozen or so cattle each, from two to four horses, and a few razorback hogs. The horses and cattle were plagued by insects and were sometimes as thin as the razorbacks. About 1897, charbon [anthrax] killed off many grass-eating animals, both domestic and wild, in Mississippi and Louisiana, and I noticed that panthers became very scarce. I suppose they had drifted to better food grounds.

At the time of attacks on people in the South, settlers were scattered, and the panther had not yet learned to fear man. The panthers were often so short of food that they even ate scraps of meat and gnawed on bones thrown away from cabins in the woods. The choosy mountain lion of the West never takes anybody's scraps.

A squad of Negro men were clearing swamp land north of Vicksburg. They noticed a panther slipping around in the woods and warned two white men, brothers, who lived in a cabin nearby. Not long afterwards while one of them was chopping wood about a hundred yards away from the cabin, he heard the other one scream. He had left him covered up in bed, shaking with a chill. He rushed to the cabin and as he went through the door was leaped upon by a panther. He had his ax but could not use it effectively. The panther escaped; it had killed the sick brother and the second one was so badly wounded that he died.

The cat family seems to have a natural taste for human flesh. While sitting up with a corpse in a house in the country, I have seen cats beg and mew in the same way they do when near a person who is dressing a chicken or a rabbit or fresh fish. House cats have been known to eat on the face of a dead person. They eat the same food that a dog eats, but a dog will give up his life guarding the body of any human being dear to him.

In 1882 Judge Henegan of West Carroll Parish in Louisiana told me this true story. A long time back a white man and an Indian set out right after dinner from a cabin on the Bayou Macon to hunt deer. It was winter time and snow was on the ground, making sign-reading easy. They stayed together for a while but saw no deer and so separated. The white man got back home about dark. When morning came and the Indian still had not showed up, he got help and went to hunt him. After trailing him about a mile from the place where the two had separated the day before, the trailers saw where the Indian had struck the tracks of a big buck deer and followed them. The trailers went on for about half a mile and found the Indian dead on the ground. Tracks made it plain that a large panther had leaped from a leaning oak tree under which he was passing, knocked him face down, apparently killing him instantly, and then rolled him over and sucked blood from his throat.

[199]

Before killing the Indian, the panther had killed the buck about sixty steps away and had sucked blood from his throat. Perhaps it scented the trailing Indian. Anyhow, tracks showed that it back-trailed the buck and waited at the leaning oak only a short time for the Indian's arrival. In making both killings the panther's tendency to jump upon a moving object seems to have been stronger than the desire to eat.

In 1888 a trapper living at Hickory Grove, Mississippi, told me of an attack that he knew of directly. It was no hearsay matter with him. Late one evening a boy fourteen years old was chopping wood near his home in the woods. His brother eleven years old was carrying the wood in. Just as this younger boy was leaning over to pick up a stick, a panther leaped upon him, knocking him to the ground. The older boy rushed upon the animal with his ax, trying to hit him, but the panther caught him. A young man who was in the stable feeding a horse heard the noise, ran out, picked up a billet of wood used to rive boards, and with it hit the panther in the head, killing it. It was not a large one. That night both boys died from their wounds, and they were buried in the same grave.

In 1906 I was at a small railroad station above Lake

Charles, Louisiana, shipping hides to the Biological Survey in Washington, D. C. There I met a very old man who was deaf, a tanner by trade. He was truthful and had a good memory. His wife kept a hotel. My hides interested him, and we talked most of the night. He related at least a half dozen instances of panthers killing early settlers around his old home in southeast Texas.

One man he told about settled with his wife and two babies near the thickets. He built a cabin and was clearing land to farm. One Saturday evening he went to a neighbor's house for something, leaving his wife burning trash and clearing up the yard in front of the cabin. It had a fence around it, and she was cleaning off the briars and cane. While she was burning a pile of trash, she heard one of the babies in the house crying. She went in and quieted it and brought the other one outside and set it down on the ground. She went on raking up trash and burning it. Then the baby on the ground began to cry. She quieted it and resumed her work.

Her back was to the baby when she heard it give a terrible squall. She looked in time to see a panther bound over the fence carrying the baby into the dense thicket just beyond. She ran after the panther, but it disappeared. At this instant the baby in the house set

[201]

up a squalling. She rushed to it, gathered it in her arms and, carrying it, ran towards the yard fence to follow the panther. The baby in her arms was still squalling. Now the panther leaped back and came towards her. She made for the house and got inside just in time to slam the door in the face of the panther. She barred it with a large slab of wood hewn for that purpose.

When the man came, he found his wife holding the bar to the door and screaming. He did not own a gun, and he ran to the neighbor's to borrow one. When he returned, the panther was reared up with his front paws on the door. He was afraid to shoot lest the bullet go through the door and kill his wife. The panther ran off into the thicket. The man now got word to the neighbors. By next morning all the men in the settlement were gathered with all their dogs. Among the men was one by the name of Paine who had a pack of hounds. They hunted every day steady for two weeks. If I remember right, it was eleven panthers they killed. They never found even a scrap of the dress worn by the baby that the panther carried off.

I could relate many instances in which a panther ate the body of a grown man, leaving only the larger bones as evidence. In some cases, the panther dragged or carried the person away still screaming and trying to fight back. Generally, as I have heard the stories, the panther started to eat on the body as soon as the person was dead.

The last panther attack that I know about directly was in the spring of 1886. I was in my camp in the Mississippi bottoms skinning a big bear I had killed when Major Hamberling, who was out on a hunt, came by to bring my mail from Smeades Station, Mississippi.

"Lilly," he said, "I almost saw a six-foot pantha on that gravel train that just passed. About eleven o'clock this morning, it sprang off the bank out of cane and caught at a Negro shoveling gravel onto a flatcar. Another Negro saw the pantha in time to hollo, and the first Negro dodged. The pantha's claws barely raked his jumper. The pantha was leaping with such speed that it struck the ground on its side instead of on its feet. Ten men loading gravel had shovels in their hands and they beat the animal down. The train conductor ran up with a pistol in his hand and shot it in the head. It was a young female."

This was not the first appearance of that panther. The preceding day the Negro that it leaped for had stepped out into the thick cane and then had run back squalling that a panther was after him. The other Negroes laughed at him and called him "Pantha." The animal seems to have picked him out of the crew for his meat; it probably remained close around the gravel pit until it made its second attack.*

* There seems to be something in the smell of certain individuals that makes them attractive to members of the cat family, just as the odor of certain people attracts dogs. Towards the beginning of this century a wildcat jumped out of the darkness one night upon a Mexican in a camp on my Uncle Jim Dobie's ranch in La Salle County, Texas. The Mexican knocked him off and he disappeared. The wildcat came back a second and a third time, leaping upon the same man — picking him out of a group of eight or ten men. Whether the wildcat had the rabies, as he was thought to have, or not, he was drawn by something distinct in the odor of the one man he attacked.

CHAPTER X

The Smell of Mortality

WHEN Ben Lilly made his talk before the
American National Livestock Association at
El Paso, in 1928, he had — without so admitting —
ceased to be very active. For decades he had followed
a system of living that would, he thought, carry him to
the century mark. While he was skinning a bear on the
Atchafalaya River in Louisiana in 1905, a doctor from
Chicago happened along, lingered with him, and told
him that a man named Henry Jenkins had lived 169
years before he died in California. A quarter of a century later, Ben Lilly, as he related in a letter to Dr. J. B.
Drake, was snowbound at the James ranch near
Chloride, New Mexico. "There were books in the
house, and I was reading at night and found a little
medical journal containing Henry Jenkins's history of
his own life. But he left no track by which another
man's life can be prolonged." Under such circumstances, the seeker after long life must make his own
tracks.

[205]

This letter, written while the sun was still bright but was about to slip below the horizon, is a revelation of the man who wrote it.

"I have been blessed in my life," he says. "I feel interested in everything that is intended for good. I have learned how to review life instead of worry. I can remember when I was a small boy. I go back to those days and bring up pleasant occurrences in my father and mother's family, and it renews my life. . . . I am proud of all my friends in all the localities I have passed through. I can recall every family that I have ever met, and it is all pleasant for me to call over. No one but myself could imagine how kindly I have been treated in the last 25 years — just a continuous journey in and through the wilds.

"I am expecting to write a book soon, describing my life from boyhood to the present day, the localities I have seen, the wild animals and wild birds. . . . I well remember how you used to take so much pains in telling me things that I would ask you questions about. I have always regarded you as a wonderful man, strictly honest, truthful and Christian. You remember I often thought you and Sam Jones [the noted evangelist] was alike. You are a natural teacher; yet you would never push yourself unless you saw it was appreciated. My eyes are A-1 yet."

It is much simpler for an individual to say "Follow Nature" than to harmonize his own very complex system with infinitely complex nature. Ben Lilly's way was often merely the way of inclination. One fall while he was a young man, in Louisiana, he took malaria. His wife managed to persuade him to see a doctor, who gave him a prescription — some decoction of quinine, no doubt. He would not take the medicine regularly; every dose he took was with growing resentment towards everybody responsible for it.

One cold morning about daybreak, the Negro cook rushed to Mrs. Lilly, exclaiming, "Jest come and looky at Mista Ben!"

Mista Ben was out wallowing in the mud. "I won't take another drop of that nasty stuff," he exploded. "I threw the bottle away. I'm going to the sulphur spring and let Nature cure me."

The sulphur spring was across the Arkansas line, twenty-eight miles away. Ben Lilly walked the distance, was gone a week, came back restored. He put some faith in native herbs. Perhaps he had been influenced by a character known all over the parish, Aunt Betsy Ross. She had been raised by Indians and in her old age went over the country administering snakeroot, teas of red oak bark, slippery elm, corn shucks and other plants. She objected to a patient's

[207]

drinking anything but her bitter teas. Ben Lilly, on the other hand, always had great faith in pure water. He would not drink ice water, but after climbing mountains afoot all day, he would walk several miles over a rough ridge into another canyon in order to camp at a cool spring, rather than stop by indifferent water. A bunch of cattle he once found alive after they had been snowed up in a canyon for sixty days with very little to sustain them except water made a strong impression on his mind.

With almost no knowledge of scientific findings on diet, and with little conception of physical complexities, he went through life advancing and dropping theories on food. He was keen in observing but weak in deducing. At one time he considered the blood of wild animals a substitute for salt. Animals, especially wild animals, were his models for diet. Observing that they make a meal off one form of food, he advocated man's making a meal from a single dish. As a table guest, he courteously ate what other people ate, but alone in his camp he generally confined his eating to corn, or corn bread, and meat. When I talked with him in 1928, he was strong on the idea that any animal, including man, after eating flesh craves whatever the animal whose flesh he has eaten feeds upon. After a lion or a bear eats deer meat, he said, it is hungry for grass, and in the same way eating fish makes a human being crave water. I did not remark that water is not fish food. He had tried eating grass like a bear, but thought that man had yet to discover the secret of the bear's health.

His eating habits are a part of the folklore of the Southwest. He cited the Bible on fasting. Like his dogs, he could trail better on an empty stomach. After a long, wearing hunt without food, his system called for food in huge amounts. So he maintained that it was beneficial to a person to fast for several days and then to gorge. He was Indian in irregularity at meals and in filling up when he had a chance.

"One time," Ed Steele recalls, "he came into our ranch after a long spell of fasting and ate enough supper to stifle a hog. At breakfast he seemed still empty. Then we started out to find a lion ranging in the country. Knowing Mr. Lilly's eating capacity, my wife had prepared a large lunch. I carried it. About a mile from the ranch house we came to a clear stream. We had not yet got well limbered up. He said 'Here would be a good place to eat our lunch.' I thought he was joking and passed off the remark lightly. We went on, and in about another mile came to another stream. Again he suggested eating lunch. I saw that he was in earnest and agreed, though I was too full to eat. We sat down; I nibbled a little, and he ate more than I would have eaten in two days. When he finished, he said, 'Now then if we jump a lion, we won't have anything to bother us.' If we had jumped one and if it had kept going for a week, he would eagerly have kept after it without another bite."

He told me that he had never been "inconvenienced" by going for days without food. "My stomach contracts," he said, "when I don't eat, and after a long fast I am not hungry until I begin working up an appetite by eating small amounts of meat or bread." The longest time he had ever gone on an exclusively meat diet, he said, was two weeks.

He regarded the lion as the most agile climber and the strongest-muscled of all animals. Therefore, lion meat should make a man supple and enable him to climb mountains and to endure. As neck muscles are particularly strong, he favored lion neck, also the neck muscles of other animals. Any wild meat was more conducive to suppleness, he thought, than meat of domestic animals. His theory that lion meat makes a man supple has been held for ages by the Apache Indians — the ancient and common theory of "transference of characteristics"; but he arrived at this theory independently. Beef he claimed made him sluggish, but he devoured great quantities of it in the

camps and homes of ranchers. At times he was raven-
ous for fat. He digested and assimilated food almost as
soon as he ate it.

When he was about sixty-two years old, he de-
veloped stomach trouble and listened to the advice
of a biologist: to vary his diet. At the same time he
went, temporarily, to the extreme of eschewing all
lion meat — a meat that many people, myself included, have found palatable.* Lion meat had given
him, he said, "that dog-gone lion fever" (pellagra).
One night in camp, Stokley Ligon heard him moving
around and the next morning mentioned the matter.
"Yes," Mr. Lilly said, "I felt sick and could not go
to sleep. For a long time I lay there wondering what
was causing the trouble. Then I remembered that lion
skin we hung up. The smell of it was making me sick.
I got up and carried it off and when I got back to my
bed, out of smell of it, I felt all right and went to
sleep."

He consulted Dr. Richard F. Stovall at Mimbres
Hot Springs. "The form of pellagra he had," Dr.
Stovall told me, "was not from the constant corn

* Among the Mountain Men "painter meat" was accounted
choicer even than beaver tail or buffalo hump, according to Chit-
tenden (*American Fur Trade of the Far West*). It was "the syno-
nym for anything particularly excellent." Also, anywhere in early-
day panther country, panther oil was reckoned as the equal of
rattlesnake oil for rheumatism.

[211]

bread or lion meat, but from not balancing his diet with fruits or vegetables. I advised him to take dried fruits with him. He did and got all right." He did not change his way of hunting, however, and that way did not regularly allow the impedimenta of selected food.

Despite abundant evidence to the contrary, some people have talked and written as if Mr. Lilly were slovenly and unclean and emitted too strong an odor to have washed. Any cow dog will tell you that a wild steer has a different odor from a tame one. Skinning lions and bears, sleeping on their hides, carrying their hides and meat on his back and eating the flesh of these animals gave the man a different aroma from that of some lettuce-eating person who regularly sleeps on fresh linen. Any healthy body emits odors that no soap will wash away and that are not unclean to natural nostrils.

M. E. Musgrave of the Biological Survey records this instance: "One Saturday night we returned from a long and strenuous hunt to our camp high in the mountains. The next morning the sun was bright, but six or eight inches of fresh snow covered the land-scape. 'Come on, let's take a bath,' Mr. Lilly called. I looked about uncertainly. More than once I had joined him in the icy waters of some mountain stream, but the little spring that supplied our camp did not afford enough water for bathing. The hardy old woodsman stripped off his clothes, seated himself in the snow, and, gathering huge handfuls of it, scrubbed himself thoroughly."

"The rancid air" in the city hotel was responsible, he was sure, for the case of pneumonia following his trip to El Paso. A cowboy drove him to the little hospital at Mimbres Hot Springs — some hot water, a few cottonwoods and cottages out in low, bleak mountains. Dr. Stovall had great difficulty keeping him in a room. He would not stay in bed. "Every morning when I rode up to the hospital," Dr. Stovall told me, "I would see Mr. Lilly hunkered under a cottonwood tree, bent over a little fire of horse manure. That little old hat would be pulled down over his eyes and his hands would be cupped around his nose and he would be inhaling the smoke from the horse manure. It was fixed in his mind that horse manure smoke would heal any respiratory trouble."

He left the hospital healed — by smoke from horse manure, or something else — and went back to the **G O S**. All forms and confinings became for him unbearable. Invited to dinner at **G O S** headquarters, where he had eaten at ease time and again, he sat down at the dining table and then suddenly said, "I just can't do it." He took a heaped plate outside and, calmly sitting on a log, ate. About this time he made himself especially odd by insisting on paying for meals at strange ranches. He found that his teeth, worn but still sound at the age of seventy-two, needed crowning. He prevailed upon dentist L. A. Jessen at the Santa Rita mines to move the chair outside the office, onto open ground, for him to sit in during the work. The "notionous" moods were increasing.

His hunts grew shorter and shorter. In the fall of 1931 two men of a hunting party that D. W. Boise accompanied saw a mountain lion not far from the G O S hunting lodge, got down off their horses and shot at it while it was running at a considerable distance up a mountain side. They reported the matter to Ben Lilly and the next morning went out with him and his dogs. At the designated spot, the dog lashed to the old hunter's waist went off at a sharp rate, almost dragging the man behind him. Mr. Lilly made it clear that he did not want company on this hunt. He came back to his camp at evening and reported that no lion had at any time recently been in that part of the range. The smell of mortality on a feebling old man who has been the strongest of the strong, the most alert of the alert, and the swiftest of the swift is the mournfulest odor on earth. And if, like King Lear, this old man will not admit that smell of mortality, what other feeling than pity is due him?

He "still looked up to sun and cloud and listened to the wind." With his dogs he would go up into a mountain and return at night, having spent the whole day gazing out from some lookout — in the manner of the big bears — into vast spaces. He was Wordsworth's Michael, who in aged desolation continued to plan a new sheepfold,

> and 't is believed by all
> That many and many a day he thither went
> And never lifted up a single stone.

He still talked about finishing the book of his life, but seemingly had no inclination to take the advice of his old and loving sister Sallie to get "some woman writer to put pep into the style and make it more catchy." "As soon as I write my book I want to go wild again," are the last words I have located on the subject, 1931.

According to one of his mountain friends, Ben Lilly "believed firmly in hell." If so, he consigned nobody to it and expected to avoid it himself. Age did not make him, to use Roosevelt's word, more "fanatical" in religion. As far as he was concerned, any man could have any kind of god he fancied, vote any ticket, or support any number of mistresses. Not even the lack of occupation in his last years drove him to the universal resort of vacant minds — gossip. Twaddle concerning the personalities of other people was out of his world. He would go his own ways without explanation; he had found those ways "very interesting." Of some ways and some people he did not approve. There was room enough on earth to avoid them; he had no call to reform them. In all his life he had had but one call. He had never tired of hunting. His mind wandered to hunting after his body could no longer follow.

He had heard of "good mountain lion range" down in Lower California. In a hope-without-faith way he talked of going to that range. He was getting so that he did not take care of himself properly. It was in these declining times that he used gunny sacks for underclothes and smelled stronger than when he had lion both inside and outside him.

At the Tom O'Brien farm-ranch on the Mimbres River, where he was persuaded to lodge, an out-room of adobe was assigned him and a woman did the cooking. He had money to pay for his keep. He was not obliged to listen to O'Brien's bragging about the bears O'Brien had killed. He made many crude knives in the blacksmith shop. A remnant of his dog pack snapped at flies around him. Now he was covering his drawings of animals with water colors such as children dabble with. He pictured red bears and purple bears. From the old green-painted breadbox in which he used to preserve his papers he would take out a blank sheet, draw a lion on it and then add a pair of buck's horns to the head.

He received urgent letters to come back to his sister's home in Mississippi. He would not leave the mountains, but now somebody had to care for him. The commissioners of Grant County, in which Silver City is situated, managed his transference to what is called the County Farm, a private property, run by Mrs. Mary Hines, on Big Dry Creek. Here he tried to make knives and then gave up trying; he drew more colored pictures. He still had the tin box for papers, but it was empty. He no longer had a dog. He would point to a tree and call to the other old men to "look at that lion up there." To one young hunter who came to visit him, he said that a man must be "accepted into the family of these Cains of the animal world and be able to speak their language" in order to hunt them successfully. He would jump across a narrow irrigation ditch. He ate what was put before him. He still wore brogans with burro shoes cleated on the heels, and, following his own tracks, he would "trail that burro." He was very tractable. He had lived for nearly eighty years, and the child in him had all that time kept childlike. He had always expected to die a hunter's death, in combat with a bear. Now he seemed indifferent to the drama of death.

One morning he told Mrs. Hines that he believed he would stay in bed. His mind seemed to lighten. He spoke about a small amount of money he had in a bank. Two hours before he breathed his last he said, "I'll be better off." He died December 17, 1936. A Methodist minister who had never seen him and had never heard of him until the day preceding conducted the funeral services. To his daughters, who came, he must have looked very strange in the coffin in Silver City, where he was buried. Somebody had shaved off his beard.

In 1947, out in the Gila National Forest, the dearest hunting range of his long life of ranging, at a site overlooking the Mogollon Mountains fifty miles away, beside a road traveled by the sparse ranch people of the country and in summertime by many tourists, J. Stokley Ligon and other friends erected a plaque to the memory of Ben V. Lilly. The bronze, imbedded in a great granite boulder, shows in bas-relief his head flanked on one side by the head of a bear and on the other side by the head of a mountain lion.

He came too late to share the "perfection of primitiveness" with Kit Carson, Jim Bridger, Broken Hand, Dick Wootton and the other Mountain Men who mapped the Rockies in their heads before cartographers mapped them on paper; but he was in the tradition of the Mountain Men and was the very last man in that tradition. There can never be another.

He was not less in stature for having been the latest. Tradition, which had already seized upon him in life, will continue to remember him apart from bronze and print. Some questions about him will remain questions. He was open; he was also closed. He was an individual; therefore he never prated about individualism. In the words of the wailing ballad of "poor Jesse James," he "came from a solitary race."

Sources: People and Print

I

In naming people who have given me oral information about Ben Lilly, sometimes bedding and feeding me to boot, who have written me letters about him and supplied pictures or other materials, I have, no doubt, unintentionally omitted some.

I must say something in particular about a few individuals. In the dedication to this book I have detailed the services of T. Y. HARP, farmer-stockman, of Morehouse Parish, Louisiana. After I had looked for the Lilly manuscripts for years, HARVEY FORSYTHE, of the Santa Rita mines in New Mexico, told me how he had rescued them, and he turned them over to me for copying. At the same time, DR. L. A. JESSEN, of Bayard, New Mexico, gave me another copy of the Lilly manuscript on lions. H. B. BIRMINGHAM, rancher of Horse Springs, New Mexico; ED STEELE, former trapper and rancher now living at North San Diego, California; CLAY HUNTER, rancher at Springerville, Arizona, who hunted with Lilly; and S. L. CARRICO, businessman at San Antonio, who as a boy camped with him — all went to the trouble to write out extensive accounts. MONROE H. GOODE of

Dallas, magazine writer on guns, hunting and game animals, who died in 1945, was an industrious collector of data on Ben Lilly. He and I exchanged much material, and I am indebted to him particularly for copies of the Lilly-McFadden correspondence and for information from Biological Survey sources.

Of all the men I have met who knew Ben Lilly, J. STOKLEY LIGON, of Carlsbad, New Mexico, seems to me to have best comprehended him. As regional supervisor for the Biological Survey work in Arizona and New Mexico, Ligon engaged Lilly to work for the Survey in 1916. A naturalist with intimate knowledge of wolves, lions, bears and other wild animals, an ornithologist and a fine gentleman as well as a man of camps, Stokley Ligon camped out with Ben Lilly, entertained him in his home, and had opportunities to know all sides of the man. In conversations and letters he has unlocked to me his knowledge, put me on the trails of other helpers, and supplied pictures. He went over the major part of my manuscript, checking for errors in fact and in deduction.

It would be interesting to me to sketch the circumstances of certain encounters; but, with a good heart, I only inscribe the names of my benefactors.

From Louisiana: STANLEY C. ARTHUR, New Orleans. MRS. M. D. L. BELL, Mer Rouge. GEORGE BOWE, Mer Rouge. HARRY BUATT, Bonita. B. P. ("PUNCH") CAUSEY, Beckman. B. C. ("BUCK") CENTERS, Pioneer. JIM COPELAND, Oak Grove. JOE DAVENPORT, Mer Rouge. L. L.

DAVIDSON, Mer Rouge. BEN GRIFFIN, Pioneer. JIM HARP, Bonita. KELLEY B. HARP, Bastrop. ROBERT E. ("SCOUT") HARP, Bastrop. T. Y. HARP, Mer Rouge. SAM HARRELL, Gallion. MRS. R. W. HOPE, Bonita. J. B. HORNBEAK, Mer Rouge. JEP HUGHES, Mer Rouge. JOHN JONES, Mer Rouge. M. E. JONES, Bastrop. JORDAN G. LEE, Jr., Dean of the College of Agriculture, Louisiana State University, Baton Rouge. CHARLIE McEALRATH, Oak Grove. MRS. R. T. McGOWEN, Bonne Idee. MRS. E. H. MILLS (sister to BEN LILLY), Shreveport. R. L. NORSWORTHY, Mer Rouge. R. W. OLDHAM, Darnell. ALONZO OLIVE, Gallion. SENATOR JOSEPH E. RANSDELL, Lake Providence. BILLY RENEAU, Oak Grove. FRANK RIVES, Mer Rouge. CALVIN G. SCOTT, Bastrop. MR. and MRS. T. B. SCOTT, Bonita. MARVIN SPENCER, Mer Rouge. CLYDE TURNER, Oak Grove. EMMET M. WHITE, Mer Rouge. JOE WHITFIELD, Lake Providence. MRS. EMMA WILLIAMSON, Bonita. DOYLE WILSON, Mer Rouge.

From New Mexico: ELLIOTT S. BARKER, Santa Fe. H. B. BIRMINGHAM, Sr., Horse Springs. JAMES K. BLAIR, Santa Rita. D. W. BOISE, Hurley. W. G. COOPER, Silver City. MRS. VICTOR CULBERSON, Lordsburg. SULTY FERMALT, Diamond Bar Ranch, Mimbres. HARVEY FORSYTHE, Santa Rita. PETE (H. C.) GIMSON, Eagle Nest. MRS. MARY HINES, Buckhorn. A. L. INMAN, Cliff. J. T. JANES, Pinos Altos. DR. L. A. JESSEN, Bayard. LOUIS H. LANEY, U. S. Fish and Wildlife Service, Albuquerque. WILL LANEY, Glenwood. J. STOKLEY LIGON, Carlsbad. DON LUSK, Silver City. MR. and MRS. JOHN MATHEWS, Santa Rita. T. HAR-

MON PARKHURST, Santa Fe. ROBERT PARSONS, Roswell. MRS. J. STONEY PORCHER, Hatch. A. D. (DOC) SEITZLER, Silver City. BLUNT SLOAN, Hot Springs. A. L. SMITH, Albuquerque. DR. RICHARD F. STOVALL (deceased), Mimbres Hot Springs. BILLY WATSON, Pinos Altos. BOYD WILLIAMS, Hope.

From Texas: S. L. CARRICO, San Antonio. CHARLES DAGGETT, Fort Worth. GEORGE V. GENTRY, University of Texas, Austin. MONROE H. GOODE (deceased), Dallas. LOCKHART HIGHTOWER, Liberty. ARDEN HOOKS, Kountze. BEN HOOKS, Kountze. HENRY H. JACKSON, Point Bolivar. TOM LEA, Sr. (deceased), El Paso. LAVOISIER LAMAR, Austin. W. H. McFADDEN, Fort Worth. EDD S. MIDGETT, Boling. W. G. PRATT, Houston. MRS. M. E. SAVAGE, Kaufman. MRS. ROBERT M. SPENCE, Palestine. E. B. STOVER, Dallas. RICHARD WALL, Dallas.

From other sections: C. G. ABBOT, Smithsonian Institution, Washington, D. C. E. C. BECKER, Springerville, Arizona. LESTER H. CHAMBERLAIN, Oceanside, California. MRS. R. CURTIS CORLEY, Cleveland, Mississippi. A. K. FISHER (deceased), Biological Survey, Washington, D. C. DORR D. GREEN, U. S. Fish and Wildlife Service, Washington, D. C. L. ALBERTO GUAJARDO (deceased), Piedras Negras, Coahuila, Mexico. JOHN D. GUTHERIE, Charlotte Court House, Virginia. CLAY HUNTER, Springerville, Arizona. CLARENCE C. INSULL, Los Angeles, California. H. H. T. JACKSON, U. S. Fish and Wildlife Service, Washington, D. C. MRS. VIRGIL LEONARD, Morenci, Arizona. JOE LILLY (cousin to BEN), Gallman, Mississippi. H. M. MERKLE,

Holly, Colorado. C. E. RANNEY, Tulsa, Oklahoma. MRS. J. H. ROGERS (deceased sister to BEN), Hazelhurst, Mississippi. H. M. SAUMENIG, Bonita, Arizona. ED S. STEELE, North San Diego, California. FRED WINN (deceased), U. S. Forest Service, Tucson, Arizona.

I I

DAY, GENE: "Old Chap Has Killed 600 Lions," *Sunday Star*, Washington, D. C., December 9, 1934.

DOBIE, J. FRANK: (1) "Mister Ben Lilly — Bear Hunter East and West," *Saturday Review of Literature*, May 16, 1942; (2) "Ben Lilly Could Read Bear Sign," *Ranch Romances*, August 3, 1943; (3) "Ben Lilly of the Mountains," *Arizona Highways*, September-October, 1943; (4) "Mister Ben Lilly in Louisiana," *Southwest Review*, Winter, 1944 (Vol. XXIX); (5) articles in *Houston Post* and other Texas newspapers (Sundays), June 10, July 4, July 18, July 25, August 8, August 29, September 5, September 12, 1943.

DUNTON, HERBERT W.: "Bear" (Ms. in University of Texas Archives).

El Paso Times (Texas), January 26, 1928: "U. S. Tariff . . . New Mexico Trapper," etc. Article, beginning on front page, reporting Ben Lilly's talk to the American National Livestock Association.

FUEHR, IRMA: (1) "The Lilly Legend," *New Mexico*, Santa Fe, January, 1943; (2) "Hunting Lions for Pay," *American Mercury*, February, 1943.

GOODE, MONROE H.: (1) "The World's Most Unique

Hunt," *Southern Sportsman*, Austin, Texas, June, 1940; (2) "The Scourge of the Livestock Country," *Cattleman*, Fort Worth, Texas, December, 1941; (3) "Ben V. Lilly, Lion Hunter of the Old Southwest," *Sports Afield*, March, 1943; (4) "Killers of the Rimrock," *Field & Stream*, June and July, 1943 — partly drawn from Lilly's manuscript on mountain lions; (5) "Ben V. Lilly," *Cattleman*, March and April, 1945.

GUTHERIE, JOHN D.: "More About Ben Lilly" (letter), *American Forests*, September, 1938.

HIBBEN, FRANK C.: "Last of the Mountain Men," *Outdoor Life*, New York, May, 1948, Vol. 101, 47–53. This article, under title of "Ben Lilly," is the first chapter of Frank C. Hibben's book, *Hunting American Lions*, Thomas Y. Crowell Co., New York, 1948. A more highly fictionized article by Hibben, "End of a Desert Bear" (in *Outdoor Life*, September, 1949), is sensationally false to man, bear and the Sierra Madre.

Illustrated World, Chicago, January, 1920: Illustration, unsigned article, "Hunting Lions in the U. S. Is His Long Suit," page 706.

LILLY, BEN V.: (1) "Famous Big Game Hunter Relates His Experiences," letter dated March 12, 1928, from Fierro, New Mexico, to J. B. Drake, Oak Grove, Louisiana, published in the *Bastrop Enterprise* (Louisiana), July 26, 1928, and reprinted in *West Carroll Gazette*, Oak Grove, Louisiana, August 3, 1928; (2) "Bears and Lions," the *Producer*, Denver, Colorado, July, 1928, and August, 1928.

(A representative of the *Producer* was at El Paso, Texas, in January, 1928, when Ben Lilly made his talk to the American National Livestock Association. The typewritten manuscripts on bears and lions that he showed me were, I understand, turned over to the *Producer*, which edited them for publication and then destroyed them.)

Lilly Manuscripts, copies in University of Texas Archives as well as in my files: *Mountain Lions of New Mexico; Mountain Lion Record, 1916* (diary); *Bears* (much mutilated); *Hunting Diary, 1922.*

Copies of Lilly letters to W. H. McFadden and to Dr. A. K. Fisher of U. S. Biological Survey, Washington, D. C.

Mammoth Western, April, 1946: "Wild Westerner" — a half-page rewrite by R. Dee.

MOULTON, ROBERT H.: "Hunting Range Varmints Is His Occupation," *Holland's Magazine*, Dallas, Texas, July, 1920.

MUSGRAVE, M. E.: "Ben Lilly — Last of the Mountain Men," *American Forests*, August, 1938.

Picayune, Daily (New Orleans): articles concerning Lilly and Roosevelt on hunt in Louisiana, October 7–21, 1907, *passim.*

RICHARDS, RAYMOND: "Veteran Hunter of Big Game Here After 54 Years on the Trail," *Denver Post*, Sunday, November 5, 1922.

RIVIERRE, RENE R., "Kills Lions for a Living," *American Magazine*, March, 1919.

[227]

ROOSEVELT, THEODORE: (1) "In the Louisiana Cane-brakes," *Scribner's Magazine*, January, 1908 (Vol. 43); (2) *Theodore Roosevelt's Letters to His Children*, edited by John Bucklin Bishop, N. Y., 1927.

Saint Louis Post Dispatch, October [about 14 or 15], 1907, "How Ben Lilly Trained His Dogs." One fourth of one column.

Shreveport Times, Louisiana, August 28, 1920: Interview with Ben Lilly, who was visiting his sister, Mrs. E. H. Mills, in Shreveport. This was his last trip east.

Silver City Enterprise, New Mexico: (1) December 25, 1936, brief account of death and burial of Ben Lilly — in which dates are wrong; (2) April 23, 1946, p. 8, "Around the Country," by Lorene Three Persons; (3) June 17, 1947, p. 4, "Memorial Plaque Will Honor Memory of Ben V. Lilly."

Ten Days in the Big Thicket of Texas. A privately made album, of which about 10 copies were distributed. Photographs by John F. Strickrott of the *Topeka State Journal* (Kansas); article dated December 15 (1906), from Kountze, Texas, evidently clipped from *Topeka State Journal*, by L. L. Kiene, editor, who made the hunt.

TEVIS, DEAN: "Ben Hooks in the Big Thicket," *Beaumont Enterprise*, Texas, February 15, 1942.

THREE PERSONS, LORENE: "Friends Erect Memorial Marker for Ben V. Lilly," *New Mexico Stockman*, August, 1947, pp. 26–27.

WINN, FRED: (1) "Ben Lilly, a Twentieth Century

Daniel Boone," *American Forestry*, July, 1923; (2) "Ben Lilly — Trapper, Mountaineer," *American Cattle Producer*, February, 1937; (3) "Ben Lilly, Lion Hunter," letter in *American Mercury*, May, 1943.

Index

Index

CPSIA information can be obtained
at www.ICGtesting.com
Printed in the USA
JSHW040016160920
7919JS00005B/13